DISCIPLESHIP PATH

GUIDING CONGREGATIONS TO CONNECT WITH JESUS

QUINCY D. BROWN

Market
Square
BOOKS

Discipleship Path

Guiding Congregations to Connect with Jesus

©2020 Quincy D. Brown

books@marketsquarebooks.com
P.O. Box 23664 Knoxville, Tennessee 37933

ISBN: 978-1-950899-11-1
Library of Congress: 2020932835

Printed and Bound in the United States of America
Cover Illustration & Book Design ©2020 Market Square Publishing, LLC

Publisher: Kevin Slimp
Editor: Kristin Lighter
Post-Process Editor: Ken Rochelle
Cover & Page Designer: Michael Buckingham

Scripture quotations are from:

CEB

Scripture quotations marked (CEV) are from the Contemporary English Version
Copyright © 1991, 1992, 1995 by American Bible Society. Used by Permission.

NIV

THE HOLY BIBLE, NEW INTERNATIONAL VERSION®, NIV®
Copyright © 1973, 1978, 1984, 2011 by Biblica, Inc.® Used by permission.
All rights reserved worldwide.

NRSV

New Revised Standard Version Bible, copyright 1989, Division of Christian Education
of the National Council of the Churches of Christ in the United States of America.
Used by permission. All rights reserved.

CONTENTS

FOREWORD

How is your congregation doing?

For the last quarter century, I have sought to help congregations by
leading workshops and training programs, serving on a seminary faculty
in leadership and ministry practice, writing articles and books, and by
coaching pastors and congregations in models and skills for church vitality. As time goes by, I have become aware that congregations are becoming
more and more concerned about their prospects for the future. Church
members often reveal decreasing confidence about having a strong church
life. Without necessarily coming right out and saying it, members seem
much more tentative about their congregations than they used to be.

What do your members talk about when they talk about your church?

Perhaps some of them talk about the weekly worship service: what
they liked about the music, whether they thought the pastor's sermon
was "a good one" or not, how inspired they felt afterward, whether a guest
or visitor sat in the same spot on the pew where that member has sat for
years, who was not there that Sunday and why.

Perhaps some of your church's members talk about its facilities—what
they really like about the sanctuary; the condition of the Sunday School
rooms; weeds growing in the parking lot or the church cemetery; how much
money it would take to repaint the fellowship hall or replace the old boiler.

Perhaps other church members like to talk about people. They might
discuss how Sadie is doing with her chemotherapy. Someone might mention how unhappy Jack and his wife have been looking lately, or those
two teenage boys who used to come to worship every Sunday without any
family, but haven't been in church for a while. The boys always sat next to
Tom, the college student who directs the youth group. People might wonder
whether the pastor has paid them a visit.

And surely some of the longtime members of your church talk aobut
memories, stories that their grandmothers told them. There were the men
who built the fellowship hall on Saturdays while the women brought in
food for grand potluck lunches. There was the dedication of the pipe organ,
after a year-long fund-raising campaign. There was Mrs. Smith, who taught

children's Sunday school classes for forty years. There were church anniversaries, July 4th cookouts, and camping trips out to the lake with campfires and singing with guitar accompaniment. Back in the day, it seemed that "everyone went to church." There were lots of families with young children.

If you were to make an educated guess, what would you say is the one hope for your church on which most of your members would agree?

My own guess would be—even though I don't think many of them would want to say it out loud—that they hope that your congregation will outlive themselves. Some might find it easier to say that they hope the building doesn't fall apart. Every once in a while, I hear a church member express confidence that their congregation will continue to have a positive influence on its community. One of the most common comments that I have heard in many congregations across the country is, "We want more families with young children."

So, what will your congregation be like ten years from now?

Some readers might have no hesitation in believing that their church will be as strong as ever. Other readers might quietly express concern that things will be tougher, with fewer members and other material resources. And then certain readers already wonder if their church will make it that long.

How does your church perceive and follow the leading of God?

Perhaps a question like this regularly guides your governing board, its officers, and your pastor. They have developed a rhythm of discussing, listening, learning, praying, and opening up collectively to divine insight and possibilities. Or, perhaps a question like this one gets little or no traction at board meetings. With so many decisions to make about bills, maintenance, supplies, fand inding volunteers, your congregation can't be bothered with something that everyone takes for granted.

What does it mean to your church to "follow Jesus?"

How would you describe your faith to another member of the congregation? How well do you see the ways in which other church members live out their faith? To what activities, relationships, or programs in the life of your congregation can you point that nurture people in their longing to be a follower of the Way? If even just one of these questions stopped you a little

2

in your tracks, gave you pause, helped you to begin thinking about your congregation more deeply, there is something in this book for you and for your congregation.

What Quincy Brown understands well is that there is more to congregational life than simply existing. Across my own lifetime, it was easy at one point to suppose that a congregation first would be organized and then continue on a successful path indefinitely. That assumption, however, can be held no longer. The conditions that made possible the rise of "church as we have known it" are fading away. You probably know this reality already, or you likely would not have picked up this book.

So, what is a congregation to do these days? The Rev. Dr. Quincy Brown—pastor, college chaplain and vice president, and now District Superintendent in The United Methodist Church—answers this question in a way that might sound simplistic to some readers, but it certainly is not. What Quincy is calling congregations to do is to recover their role as disciple-makers. Instead of congregants wishing that new people just might "come to our church," Brown reminds us that the Church has a job to do.

How can congregations effectively proclaim and celebrate Good News, feed hungry people, support those who are ill and grieving, and seek justice in a troubled world, if persons are not shown how to do so? Indeed, as Dr. Brown will tell you, the word "disciple" in the New Testament can be translated also as "pupil" or "apprentice." Pupils are people who put themselves in a position from which they can learn something valuable from someone with those particular skills. In this case, the "someone" is the congregation and its members.

If you are ready to help your congregation in the challenging, yet rewarding, work of nurturing people for a life of Christian faith and action, keep reading. There is plenty in this book to guide you and encourage you. Oh, and don't be surprised if you realize along the way that your congregation discovers unexpected joys. The experience of Spirit-led transformation has a way of doing that!

Ready? Roll up your sleeves, start praying, keep listening, keep learning, and work together. Through it all, God will bring blessing.

George B. Thompson, Jr., Ph.D.
Co-Founder and Co-Director
The Vibrant Congregations Initiative

ACKNOWLEDGMENTS

I want to thank all of the people who made this project possible and encouraged me to write this book. I am thankful for Steve Dodson, who first challenged me to develop a path for church engagement while I served as his executive pastor. The engagement path was the precursor to the *Discipleship Path*. I am grateful to F. Douglas Powe, Jr., the Director of the Lewis Center for Church Leadership at Wesley Theological Seminary, who planted the seed for me to write this book.

I appreciate Shonnie Scott's monthly ZOOM calls that motivated the structure of this book. Her invaluable affirmation and guidance allowed me to create a tangible way to connect people with Jesus. I owe an ongoing debt of gratitude to my administrative assistant and office administrator, Renee Farrar, without whom nothing on my task list would get done.

It is a blessing to work with an incredible group of pastors who represent fifty-six churches in the Atlanta Decatur Oxford District (which includes nearly 800,000 people and covers three and one-half counties), my assigned area as a Superintendent and chief missional strategist. Through several workshops, these pastors and their members helped to shape this work into the book you see today. I also owe a debt of gratitude to the pastors and laypeople of the Baltimore Washington Conference of The United Methodist Church and to Rodney Smothers for providing feedback of improvement for *Discipleship Path*. I also want to acknowledge Jonathan DeWaal and Ron Carucci of Liminal Space for inviting me to participate in a year-long in-depth cohort to become a transitional guide. Working with them taught me the importance of *discerning, dreaming,* and *developing* a process for transitions and change.

I am equally indebted to the coaching cohort led by George and Beverly Thompson, founders and directors of The Vibrant Congregations Initiative, for their inspiration provided by their books *Futuring Your Church, Ready to Lead,* and *Grace for the Journey.* Both cohort experiences sparked my imagination to create a process to guide congregations in making the transition from an exclusively insider focus to moving outside their walls.

A special thanks go to Ralph Thompson, Yvette Massey, Jan McCoy,

Cassie Rapko, and Deanne Lynch, who served on the 3D Journey Design Team. The team helped me to create the workshop training that led to this book. Several more friends provided the necessary support while writing this book. I am grateful to Stuart Gulley, Shonnie Scott, Beverly and George Thompson, and Olu Brown for their proofreading and suggestions.

I extend my heartfelt gratitude to Michael Buckingham of **Holy Cow Marketing** for designing the book. I am thankful for Kevin Slimp and the staff of Market Square Publishing Company for allowing me to publish *Discipleship Path*. I owe a debt of gratitude to Jan McCoy for her patience and editorial skills. Her work with the manuscript enabled me to say my thoughts with clarity. I am grateful for our collaboration.

Finally, I want to recognize, thank, and celebrate the love of my life, my wife, Dionne, for her partnership over the years. Without her, the ministry would be incredibly difficult. I love you, and I am grateful for your life-long devotion and support.

INTRODUCTION

You have shown me the path to life, and you make me glad by being near to me.

Psalms 16:11 (CEV)

...Two roads diverged in a wood, and I—I took the one less traveled by, and that has made all the difference.

Robert Frost[1]

Eric and Greg were the two most influential relatives of my childhood. Eric was six years older, and Greg was three years older than me. Eric lived fifty miles away, but would frequently visit his grandmother, who was our next-door neighbor and one of my Mama's four sisters. Greg, grandson of another of Mama's sisters, lived a few minutes away. They both provided a "path" to follow. I wanted to imitate Eric, but Greg, who was closer in age and nearer in proximity, had more of an influence on me.

Periodically, Mama would drop off my brother and me at Greg's house to play. During those visits, Greg, his brother, my brother, and I were inseparable. Greg was the trickster ringleader of the group, and he made up silly games for us to play. Many of those games required us to imitate his actions. One game we played was "strikeout," Greg's version of front-porch baseball.

By creating the game, Greg demonstrated how to stand, where to throw the ball, and how hard to swing so the ball would not break a window. As a good physical trainer does, he demonstrated the techniques, and we followed in his footsteps. Before long, we began to master "strikeout," and he moved us to the backyard to play "real" baseball, where he was the umpire.

In addition to guiding us in made-up games, Greg would also tell us outlandish stories that bordered on make-believe. He was the first to tell

---

[1] Robert Frost, "The Road Not Taken," *Mountain Interval* (New York: Henry Holt and Company, 1916), 9.

me about the "haunted path." Due to his prankish ways, I did not believe him until I heard other neighborhood kids say something similar about the well-traveled trail in the neighborhood.

Etched in the middle of a grassy field where the Northwestern School, a private school built by the Northwestern Baptist Association to educate black children, once stood, the path was legendary. The rumor around the neighborhood was that when the school was operational, some of the old pianos stored on the stage in the auditorium would play themselves. The story was that murders went unsolved on the site, and the deceased haunted the campus.[2] The "haunted" auditorium was torn down, but somehow or other, the haunts remained. Without a building to roam, the ghosts supposedly shifted to the nearby path. The story of the haunted path gained so much power that no one dared to walk through it after nightfall!

There were other paths in the neighborhood, including the one that cut through the brush and debris adjacent to Greg's neighbors' house. This path led to the unused railroad tracks and required us to clear it of unsightly thorny brier patches and kudzu. When we were not walking the path, we walked "the tracks" to Latimer's store to buy cookies. My favorite was Uncle Al's Old Fashion Stage Planks Cookies, and Greg's favorite was Jack's Cookies.

Despite the many times that we walked the tracks, the path remained the "main road" for us to walk, play, and ride our bikes. Though haunted at night, in the daytime, it was a place for mischief, adventure, and storytelling. The path was our place to tell past and future stories to pass the time.

As we got older and started to drive, the magic hold of the path diminished. Somewhere during this transition to adolescence, Greg went to college, and life was no longer the same. We tried to imitate how Greg would do things, but we were unable to recreate the ringleader's magical appeal. After Greg's family moved from Newtown, we did not visit the path or the neighborhood as frequently. It was also during this time that I rekindled my desire to be like Eric.

On one particular visit, Eric met with me to inquire about my plans. His grandmother told him that I wanted to be just like him. He asked, "Are you going to college?" I replied, "No, my counselor and teachers said that I wasn't college material." Empathetically, Eric urged me to reconsider

---

[2] I am indebted to my relative Jerry Castleberry for sharing the history of the Northwestern School and the pass. By the time my generation came of age, the term "pass" had made a shift to "path."

going to college. As a star-struck teenager filled with hero worship, I was unaware of the long hours he worked to maintain the cars and clothes I admired. He told me, "Cuz, I want a better path for you. I want you to do better than I did."

Eric revealed how hard he had to work at a local factory. He expressed that "No one should have to work so hard to earn a decent wage." A few years later, I would see the toll of the long, hard hours on him as I moved in to live with him during my college years. Because of his grueling work schedule, I rarely saw Eric during the week. Now, some many years later, I have been thinking about my life with Greg and Eric in a different way. Eric had encouraged me to seek a better path, so I did. The path called for a lot of commitment on my part: time, energy, study, and patience. Looking back, I am grateful for Eric's encouragement; it made a big difference for my life and ministry.

Just as Eric wanted a better path for me, I want a better path for your church. In the same way that we stopped using the neighborhood path, I am concerned that many churches have stopped growing and are also experiencing a significant decline in participation and attendance. Whether it is a shrinking choir, diminishing weekly offerings, or not enough children in worship to do a children's sermon, many churches are struggling. Now more than ever, the church needs a better path that leads to revitalization— the renewal of life that Jesus promised his disciples.

Following the path of revitalization will offer your church the opportunity to live out the gospel message of connecting people with Jesus. Revitalizing your church will take a significant investment of time, energy, resources, and laser-focus. Understandably, many churches will want to turn things around quickly. But when the emphasis is on speed, the revitalization process is severely compromised, and will be eventually stalled to a halt. This may sound obvious, but if you want to see change in your church, the way that you do church in the future has to be different from what your church is doing today. As we will see throughout this book, revitalization is no small task. It requires the hard work of intentionally charting a better path[3] for charting a better path also hints that any time

---

[3] Both Will Mancini's and Tony Morgan's work influences my understanding of helping churches to map out a discipleship path with a priority for the next steps. See Will Mancini and Warren Bird, God Dreams: 12 Vision Templates For Finding and Focusing Your Church's Future (Nashville: B & H Publishing Group, 2016); and Tony Morgan, The Unstuck Church: Equipping Churches to Experience Sustained Health (Nashville: Thomas Nelson, 1989/2017).

something new is started, something old must come to an end. Because this book presents a new way of thinking about discipleship for many churches, readers will need to make a transition from the familiar way of thinking by enduring a time of *discernment, dreaming,* and *development* to begin something new.

FOUNDATIONAL PRINCIPLES

This book will show your church how to make the transition to a *discipleship path.* Here, we focus on where to begin in the process by shifting from an insider to outsider focus, streamlining existing programs for missional alignment, and celebrating small and large wins along the way. The concept of discipleship, from my perspective, is fundamentally connected to an exodus transition of how people leave an old status and struggle to determine what it means to be in a new relationship with God.[4]

For our work together, the Exodus story will serve as the first of two foundational principles that influence my definition of discipleship. I will refer to several episodes from the Exodus story throughout the book. The second and most important principle is on Jesus' emphasis to "Follow me, and I will make you fish for people" (Matthew 4:19). I believe that following Jesus' command to fish for people requires embracing practices that help people to:

- Give attention to God's presence by participating in worship.
- Serve inside and outside the church walls.
- Grow through Bible study and prayer.
- Invest time, talent, and financial gifts to support the church's mission.
- Make an impact that demonstrates a faithful witness of what it means to follow Jesus.

These characteristics[5] provide the outcomes of discipleship and answer

---

[4] Allen Coppedge, The Biblical Principles of Discipleship (Wilmore: Francis Asbury Press, 2017), 17.

[5] Both Phil Maynard and James Harnish's works influence my notion of using the vows of United Methodist membership as practices for discipleship outcomes. See Phil Maynard, *Shift 2.0: Helping Congregations Back into the Game of Effective Ministry* (Knoxville: Market Square Books, LLC, 2019), 5; and James A Harnish, *A Disciple's Path Daily Workbook: Ministry in the Small Membership Church* (Nashville: Abingdon Press, 2012), Kindle Edition, Location 107.

the question, "What does a disciple do?" They also provide a path that moves people toward Christlike transformation. The outcomes always involve the transition to follow Jesus' way of suffering on the cross (life in Egypt), death (the wilderness), and resurrection (new life in Promised Land).

Just as the Israelites suffered from the emergence of a new king who did not favor them, our churches also find themselves in a culture where regular church attendance is no longer preferred. More precisely, our churches remain unclear on how to navigate the new world where the goal is not to find a place, but to experience the promise of transformation. Churches are unaware that the solution to decline and plateau is discovered through the process of *discerning, dreaming,* and *developing* a *discipleship path* to fulfill the mission of making disciples.

HOW TO USE THIS BOOK

From what you have read so far, you may be thinking, "Okay, Quincy, we can see that you are going to tell us about a process we can follow that will turn things around. But will this process help us?" Yes, but not entirely in the way that you may be thinking. This book is not one where I tell you the answers. Instead, this book helps you to clear new paths for new life through discipleship for the long haul.

I wrote this book to help your church with the question: How can I help your church adapt to your current context to reinvent and revitalize yourselves in and for a new time? Written for the local church, I wanted to create a book that the average layperson can pick up and immediately apply. Like the Apostle Paul's work in Athens of sharing The Good News of Jesus Christ in a different culture, your church is encouraged to do the same (Acts 17:16-22). You must learn to connect Athens (life outside the church walls) with Jerusalem (life inside the church). The goal is to catch the missionary spirit of engaging the culture outside your walls to connect people with Jesus.

In the process, I will invite you to spend considerably more time in sharing your stories, the most difficult ones, along with the stories that tell the best of what you do. Both types of accounts will reveal your church's culture: the stories that emerge from the beliefs, assumptions, shared practices, and traditions you hold dear. As you review your stories, you will

11

discover that your traditions create nostalgia, the residue from previous success stories that no longer work today. When you begin to sort through your church's culture, be ready to address the outlandish "ghost" stories of unexamined assumptions and submerged beliefs. Submerged beliefs represent assumptions that are not particularly religious in nature. Assumed to be true, and often in non-negotiable ways, submerged beliefs focus on the nature of time, truth, relationships, resources, and power, will influence both individual and group dynamics, and will haunt you when poked or stirred.

You will recognize such "ghost" stories as the ones that hold a lot of energy[6], but they are the elephant in the room. Everyone will know it is there, but no one will want to discuss it. Stories of fires, affairs, embezzlement, and large blocks of members leaving for one reason or another are just a few of the factors that frame the ghost stories that you might encounter. Until you face your ghost, it will be like Jacob Marley's tormented ghost roaming the earth without solace.[7]

Throughout the book, I will highlight different churches as examples. All of the church stories are from my encounters over twenty-five years of ministry. The stories are composites of several churches that I encountered over the years, and for the sake of anonymity, I have altered the names and circumstances. The people are composites from countless conversations with people outside of the church walls that I have encountered during my tenure as a district superintendent. The names are changed, but the case studies are real.

The book is written in two parts. In Part One, "Clearing the Path," we will look at three churches and their attempts to clear a path. Chapter 1 introduces the concept of discipleship, and Chapters 2 and 3 introduce the importance of guidance and engagement. Chapter 4 will look at a rural church struggling with discerning how to increase worship attendance. In Chapter 5, we delve into the insights learned from the rural church's experiences and offer concepts and practices for your church.

---

[6] Submerged beliefs are the hidden sources of the energy that control a congregation. They represent the deeply held convictions which, although never spoken aloud, a church takes for granted. See Beverly A. Thompson and George B. Thompson Jr., *Grace for the Journey: Practices and Possibilities for In-Between Times* (Herndon: The Alban Institute, 2011) Kindle Edition location 1008.

[7] See Charles Dickens' *A Christmas Carol In Prose Being: A Ghost Story of Christmas*, 1859 Edition, (New York: Global Classics, 2014).

In Chapter 6, we will follow a suburban church's struggle to *dream* about how to turn around financial giving. Chapter 7 will zoom in on themes highlighting the suburban church's *dream* process to address declining participation in its programs.

Chapter 8 focuses on an urban church looking to help its members develop strategies to serve its changing community. Turning to Chapter 9, we take an in-depth look at how the urban church will develop action steps to make a positive impact by addressing community issues. At the end of these chapters, I alternate between questions and spiritual practices.[8]

Part Two, "Walking the Path," provides exercises to help you and your church walk the path of discipleship. This section of the book is akin to a workbook where your church will experiment with the discipleship path. The last five chapters (10-14) are case studies designed to assist your congregation in *discerning, dreaming,* and *developing* practices unique to your context for five composite characters living near your church. Each chapter in Part Two will look at the areas of worship, serve, grow, give, and impact, and create an engagement process to help your congregation reach the goals of discipleship.

For our work together, we will name The United Methodist vows of membership (Presence, Service, Prayers, Gifts, and Witness) as the goals of discipleship.[9] As you read, resist the temptation to skip to Part Two before your team has completed Part One. I have deliberately included images, metaphors, and biblical stories to invoke your congregation's ability to *discern, dream,* and *develop* your way of clearing and walking a discipleship path. If you choose to use this book as a group, the entire process can take up to nine-months to complete (at minimum, four months to engage in the questions and practices in the "Clear the Path" section and five months to engage in the practices in the "Walk the Path" section). I look forward to walking with you on the path.

---

[8] At the end of these chapters, I alternate between questions and spiritual practices to help guide your team in clearing a path to discern, dream and develop an attitude of intentional awareness that opens you more deeply to who you are and whose you are as a community of faith called by God to make an impact on the world. For more information on spiritual practices, see Dorothy C. Bass, editor, *Practicing Our Faith: A Way of Life for a Searching People* (San Francisco: Jossey-Bass, 1997); and Diana Butler Bass, *The Practicing Congregation: Imagining a New Old Church* (Herndon, VA: The Alban Institute, 2004).

[9] Harnish, Kindle Edition, Location 223.

PART ONE
Clearing the Path

Is **your church** creating a path for people to connect with Jesus and inviting others to walk the same way? Or is your church process unwittingly designed to walk people in a loop to come back to the starting point without any change? Asking questions and listening to congregational stories are the foundation for clearing a path.

In this section, we will focus on what it means for your church to clear a path for your members to walk towards community engagement, health, and vitality. I will discuss ways your church can identify and make a path to engage people. We will look at the three types of congregations: rural, suburban, and urban ones. With each group, we explore how they engage the areas of worship, serve, grow, give, and impact on addressing the decline.

1

DISCIPLESHIP

Connecting People with Jesus

Go therefore and make disciples of all nations, baptizing them in the name of the Father and of the Son and of the Holy Spirit, and teaching them to obey everything that I have commanded you.

Matthew 28:19-20a (NRSV)

The mission of the church is to go into the world in the power of the Spirit and make disciples by proclaiming this gospel...[10]

Matthew Barrett

Discipleship is about connecting people with Jesus. Discipleship is a life-long journey that is messy where none of us ever fully arrive. It is the mission of the church that focuses on both the personal and communal aspects of life. George Barna offers a description that helps to define what it means to connect people with Jesus. In his book, *Growing True Disciples,* his definition includes a life-change process of accepting Jesus as Savior and Lord to alter a person's values, goals, and relationships. He describes discipleship as:

---

[10] Trevin Wax, "Defining The 'Mission' of the Church," accessed October 19, 2019. https://www.thegospelcoalition.org/blogs/trevin-wax/defining-the-mission-of-the-church/.

...becoming a complete and competent follower of Jesus Christ. A person is seeking others who are serious about becoming new creations in Christ – individuals who are fanatics, zealots, mesmerized, passionate about the cause, wholly devoted to mimicking their model down to the last nuance. Discipleship is not a program. It is not a ministry. It is a lifelong commitment to a lifestyle.[11]

Barna's description also includes the importance of attending Bible study and small groups. But as important as learning scripture and Christian fellowship might be, it is not the full description of discipleship. A closer look reveals that a disciple is someone who connects with Jesus to walk a path that imitates his life, practices, and teachings.

With a few exceptions, most churches, as I have discovered, do not struggle with the definition of a disciple. By contrast, however, most churches struggle with how to make a disciple. How does church life, that is, the way that you do church, embody the promise of life-change for a

DISCIPLESHIP INVOLVES ANALYSIS, LEARNING FROM JESUS' TEACHINGS, AND ACTION, PUTTING THE LESSONS INTO PRACTICE.

changing community longing for hope? Expressed a bit differently, the Bible commands us to make disciples, but it does not give us a "cookie-cutter" answer on how to do it. And when we get down to it, the process of how to make a disciple in your church becomes the arduous task that can be intimidating, impossible, and outright confusing.[12] As difficult as it may be to make disciples, if we are given a little time, I suspect that we all can name existing disciples in our churches. For instance, I can provide several names of disciples from my home church. I am sure that you can

---

[11] George Barna, *Growing True Disciples: New Strategies for Producing Followers of Christ* (Colorado Springs: Waterbrook Press, 2001), 19, 27-28.

[12] Dana Yeakley, *The Gentle Art of Discipling Women: Nurturing Authentic Faith in Ourselves and Others* (Colorado Springs: NavPress, 2015), 170

do the same with your church.

During several encounters with different churches in my work as district superintendent,[13] I have developed the practice of asking the pastor if he or she knows the stories of how the members became disciples. Most of the pastors were not able to answer the question. Instead, several pastors sheepishly told me that this was not a question that came to mind while working with church people. Instead, most of them reported spending the majority of their focus on attendance, finances, programs, and caring for the members. Here are some of the responses that the pastors reported and my interpretation of what I heard.

What the pastor said: We used to have two hundred kids in Sunday school. Today, it is about sixty.

What the people were unknowingly asking: How do we convince parents with kids in soccer, band, tennis, and baseball to prioritize attending church?

What the pastor said: Families attend our events like Trunk or Treat, BBQs, and Back to School Activities, but they don't come to church.

What the pastor and people did not acknowledge: Our church has no clue how to connect with people moving into our community. We don't know them, and they don't know us.

As unsettling as what this story-inventory reveals, it is obvious to me (and perhaps to you, too) that for churches to fulfill their mission, they must give more attention to the work of making disciples.

The step-by-step process of clearing and walking a discipleship path will help to answer the question of how a person becomes a disciple.

---

[13] A district superintendent is a clergy appointed by a bishop to select clergy to oversee the administrative processes of providing strategic, spiritual, and pastoral leadership to the churches in a geographical region called a district. For more information, see http://www.umc.org/who-are-we/districts.

TO MAKE A DISCIPLE, YOU MUST BE CLEAR ABOUT
THE PRACTICES AND GOALS OF DISCIPLESHIP. IN A
NUTSHELL, THE PEOPLE IN YOUR PEWS WILL NEED A
STEP-BY-STEP PROCESS THAT HELPS THEM IMITATE
HOW TO LOVE GOD AND TO LOVE OTHERS.

CLEAR THE PATH, WALK THE PATH

Clearing and walking along the path of becoming a disciple involves asking questions and listening to your church's stories, which will help you explore your beliefs, behaviors, and assumptions about how to live. Further, clearing and walking a discipleship path represents the adaptive work of asking questions and listening to the community's stories outside the church walls.

For practical purposes, it might be helpful to see the process of the discipleship path as a 3D-Journey where the D's stand for *Discern, Dream, and Develop*.[14] **Discern (Praying)**: Prayerfully, make a deep dive into your church's past success stories, looking especially for patterns. This is a deliberate process that involves asking, seeking, and knocking to hear the stories that make your church tick and how these stories affect the people who attend it (Matthew 7:7). After you hear the stories, I encourage you to discuss ways to acknowledge and appreciate what has shaped your traditions and behavior. Every church will have these stories, especially the ones that date back to times when the sanctuary and the Sunday school classrooms were full. Looking at these stories can help your church find its way forward to *dream* again. Discerning questions are "Why" questions that unearth core stories of more significant meaning and profound energy residing just below the surface of people in the congregation's action.

Dream (Brainstorming): Imagining the glimpses of God's good and pleasing preferred future picture for your church (Romans 12:2) is

---

[14] There are parallel resources that follow a similar path. For more information See Mark Lau Branson, *Memories, Hopes, and Conversations: Appreciative Inquiry and Congregational Change* (Herndon: The Alban Institute, 2004); and Rebekah Simon-Peter, *Dream Like Jesus: Deepen Your Faith and Bring the Impossible to Life* (Knoxville: Market Square Books, 2019).

accomplished by using the success stories of the past that are unique to the church. The *dream* phase of the process requires a leap of faith and trusting God to see visions and dreams (Acts 2:7). Dream questions are "What if?" questions that help to imagine future possibilities of the discerning stories. For example, your church might ask the following "what if" question: "What if our church became the place that provides processes, teachings, and activities to help parents and grandparents apply biblical principles successfully so that their children and grandchildren navigate the pressures of adolescence?"

Develop (Planning for Action): Uses the stories of the past and dreams for the future to create a plan of action for what can be. Develop questions are "how" questions that develop strategies to implement the *dream*. This includes sitting down to "count the cost" (Luke 14:28) of time and resources to accomplish the plan.

We will be using the *discern, dream,* and *develop* process in more detail in Part Two, "Walking the Path," as we look at helping five people on the discipleship path. You will want to refer back this section to refresh your thoughts about the process as you walk along the discipleship path.

WALK THIS WAY

In their book *Sitting at the Feet of Rabbi Jesus,*[15] authors Ann Spangler and Lois Tverberg provide a pop-culture reference that illustrates another aspect of discipleship. When discussing "imitation" as a vital practice of discipleship, they refer to a scene in the 1974 comedy-horror film *Young Frankenstein.*[16] In the scene, a hunched-back servant named Igor (played by bug-eyed Marty Feldman) meets young Dr. Frankenstein (played by Gene Wilder), the grandson of the infamous mad-scientist Victor Frankenstein, at a train station in Transylvania. When Igor comically hobbles down the steps, he instructs Frankenstein to "walk this way." The young Frankenstein then literally hunches over and lurches down the steps mimicking Igor's every move.

---

[15] Ann Spangler and Lois Tverberg, *Sitting at the Feet of Rabbi Jesus: How the Jewishness of Jesus Can Transform Your Faith* (Grand Rapids: Zondervan, 2015), 55.

[16] *Young Frankenstein*, directed by Mel Brooks, featuring Gene Wilder, Peter Boyle, Marty Feldman, Cloris Leachman, and Teri Garr (Universal City: Universal Pictures, 1974).

As a member of Generation X (born in 1969), I am captured by another image of imitation: Run-DMC's 1985 video "Walk This Way" featuring Aerosmith. The video begins showing practice sessions for Run-DMC and Aerosmith. The rap trio is frustrated with Aerosmith's significant guitar riffs that are bleeding through the wall that separates the two groups' rehearsal spaces. Irritated by not being able to hear their own music, Run-DMC turns their speakers towards the wall and plays the "Walk This Way" record. Thinking that it is his band playing when Tyler begins to sing, Run-DMC abruptly interrupts him to rap the lyrics over him.

Eventually, the groups "clear a path to walk together," where Run-DMC raps the verses, and Tyler sings the iconic chorus. Near the end of the video, the lead singer of the rock band imitates the dance steps of Run-DMC, the shell-toed-Adidas-sneakers-without- shoestring-wearing rappers from Hollis Queens.

It is fitting that the inspiration for Aerosmith's song *Walk This Way* is the film *Young Frankenstein.* According to the Wall Street Journal author Marc Myers' report,[17] the band suffered writer's block during the production of their forthcoming album, Toys in the Attic, and went to see Young Frankenstein in Times Square. Laughing from the "walk this way" scene, the band's director and Tyler made it the title for their song. Both the images from the film and video capture the follow-the-leader emphasis of imitation that I first experienced with my cousin Greg. A path of imitating the leader is the type of discipleship we find in Jesus' time.

FIRST-CENTURY DISCIPLESHIP AND TODAY

The first-century Jewish world of Jesus also influences the imitation emphasis of discipleship. During that time, a disciple followed a rabbi to master the rabbi's teachings. The purpose was to imitate and practice the way the rabbi lived, prayed, studied, taught, served, and bore witness to a close relationship with God.

Learning was not about retaining information as much as gaining

---

[17] Marc Myers, "How Aerosmith Created 'Walk This Way': A look at how the hard-rock band, inspired in part by 'Young Frankenstein,' came up with a song that would become a top-10 hit twice." *The Wall Street Journal.* Archived from the original on March 10, 2015. Retrieved October 22, 2019.

wisdom for living through hands-on experiences. Learning as a disciple meant imitating a teacher who possessed the skills the student wanted to acquire.[18] A disciple was expected to become like the rabbi. So, when Jesus says, "Come, follow me, and I will send you to fish for people"(Matthew 4:19) and "Go and make disciples" (Matthew 28:19), he is inviting and commanding them to become and make a *mathetes* (math-e-tees), the Greek word which means "an attached follower of a teacher's life." Jesus' disciples were to find new followers who would connect people with the application of Jesus' teachings and way of life.[19] The disciples' task was to connect people with Jesus.

For many in our congregations, connecting people with Jesus means teaching them beliefs about God and accepting Jesus as Lord, and educating them in doctrinal truth. Though essential, this method approaches the gospel primarily as information that is transmitted and received. But knowledge alone will not transform lives.

In their book *Resurgence,* Candace Lewis and Rodney Smothers highlight the transformative nature of discipleship:

Growing churches understand [that] discipleship is the church's primary role, not just membership. Focusing on membership alone will not connect churches with their expanding mission field.[20]

Following Lewis' and Smothers' work, it becomes clear that decline and stagnation in churches is not the primary problem. Instead, the problem lies in whether or not the church understands discipleship as its central focus. This shift in focus represents a challenge for some churches to embrace initially. When I ask church leaders to consider discipleship as the primary role, many respond with a curious look and ask more questions:

- **Aren't discipleship and membership the same thing?**
- **How long does it take to become a disciple?**

---

[18] Spangler and Tverberg, 57-58.

[19] Yeakley, 71.

[20] Candace M. Lewis and Rodney Thomas Smothers, *Resurgence: Navigating the Changing Ministry Landscape* (Berwyn Heights: Heritage Publishing, 2019), 138.

• **Do we have to change anything?**

These responses are not to criticize churches. On the contrary, these responses recognize the church's need for a clear path of discipleship. A closer look at the practices of many churches will reveal that a more deep-seated need for guidance exists within churches to move them away from an exclusive focus on membership and toward discipleship. To be sure, making disciples is different from making members.[21] In the next chapter, we will focus on how your church can guide your team and congregation in the process of making disciples.

QUESTIONS FOR INDIVIDUAL REFLECTION

1. What are the stories that have informed how the members of your church became disciples?

2. In your own words, how would you define a disciple of Jesus?

[21] Gilbert R. Rendle, *Journey in the Wilderness: New Life for Mainline Churches* (Nashville: Abingdon Press, 2010), 12.

3. What are the beliefs and behaviors that you would name as essential for a disciple of Jesus?

2

GUIDING CONGREGATIONS

Navigating Change and Transitions

There the angel of the Lord appeared to him in a flame of fire out of a bush; he looked, and the bush was blazing, yet it was not consumed.

Exodus 3:2 (NRSV)

If we don't encounter liminal space in our lives, we start idealizing normalcy. The threshold is God's waiting room. Here we are taught openness and patience as we come to expect an appointment with the divine Doctor.[22]

Richard Rohr

To make a disciple requires that someone is available to guide the process. Most congregations look to their pastors for this guidance. Sadly, the leadership skills needed to initiate and guide the disciple-making process represents a significant shift for many pastors and their congregations. For all practical purposes, the powers that most pastors have been taught or have "caught" are generally inadequate for this challenge.

---

[22] Richard Rohr, Center for Action and Contemplation, "Liminal Space," accessed October 26, 2019, https://cac.org/liminal-space-2016-07-07/.

Without the knowledge and skills needed to help guide congregations, many will become overwhelmed and give up. To help you keep the potential feelings of despair at bay, I will focus on the underlying concepts in this chapter that will help you guide your congregation along the discipleship path. A guide for the process is necessary since, as we saw in Chapter 1, how the church goes about making a disciple is not the first question that most pastors ask when they are assigned to a church. It may seem daunting, but do not be discouraged. I believe you can learn the skills and knowledge it takes to guide your congregation to connect people with Jesus.

If your congregation is going to rely on the pastor to guide it through a disciple-making process, then your congregation may need to make a shift in theory and practice. Such a shift will require that your church manage the anxiety-ridden season of transition to make space for a new approach. Likewise, if you are a pastor who wants to help your congregation make disciples, then you will need to unlearn what you know about leadership and adapt your practices. Finally, if you are a layperson and you want to be part of a team to help guide your congregation in making disciples, you will need to learn new skills. In any case, both pastors and laity will need to be prepared for a lengthy journey of learning what it means to guide people through the transition process of making disciples.

THE WAY OF TRANSITION

Like the lenses in my glasses that seamlessly adapt to the changing light, from clear indoors to bright outdoors and every shade in between, a transition is the emotional re-centering that we all must go through to make change work. And contrary to popular belief, the shift does not start with a new situation, but rather the shift starts when we can let go of our old status. The most accessible example of a transition available to us is found in the life of Moses and the Israelite exodus from Egypt.

Before Moses' time, in the days of Joseph, his people had lived in Egypt contentedly and held considerable power. By the time Moses was born, the Egyptians had enslaved his people. Moses did what any good transitional guide does: He looked for ways to force the old system to release its grip and to "let my people go." He discovered that it is difficult to break a system's hold on people. And as usual, with any transition, plagues of problems begin to develop.

Today, the "plagues" that affect your church are more metaphorical, but the message conveyed by the diseases is always the same: "We have never done it this way before, but the old ways are not working anymore." As we read in Exodus, whatever the old system is, it always "follows" you and tries to pull you back, just as the Pharaoh's army followed the Israelites in an attempt to take them back to Egypt. In the church world, the old way represents time-worn values, outdated processes, symbols, and ceremonies that exert a hold on people.

The "old system" follows you in a variety of ways. Perhaps it is a worship style, a particular fellowship event, or a long-tenured and beloved staff person's way of doing things that tug at our heartstrings and makes letting go so difficult. When you experience this heartstring tug, is an indication that change is ahead and you are on the edge of the wilderness of uncertainty. And while people will react to the wilderness in different ways, wilderness always follows the familiar, idealizing (and perhaps idolizing) the way things "used to be." In Exodus, the Israelites romanticized their former life in Egypt and began to murmur:

What was so bad about Egypt, anyway? Do you think Moses knows where he's going? I'd never signed up for this if I knew it was going to be like this!

Moses could not get his people into the Promised Land, so the tradition goes, until the ones who had known Egypt had died. If we take that literally, it is a pretty discouraging message. But if we take it symbolically, it suggests that the old attitudes and behaviors that were appropriate for Egypt must die to generate new ones, or else the Promised Land will prove to be just a modern Egypt.

Every church will experience murmuring in the transition process. Put another way, when people begin to complain about things in your church, it is a sure sign that transition is afoot. And if you are going to guide your church through its wandering wilderness season, you will need to develop the skills to remain centered in the face of complaining and acting out. Again, Moses provides for us an example of what not to do by allowing our frustration to get the best of us. During a water crisis in the wilderness, Moses' failure in how he reacted to the murmuring of the Israelites caused him to act out and strike the rock instead of speaking to it, as God commanded:

Now there was no water for the community, and the people gathered in opposition to Moses and Aaron. They quarreled with Moses and said, "If only we had died when our brothers fell dead before the Lord! Why did you bring the Lord's community into this wilderness, that we and our livestock should die here? Why did you bring us up out of Egypt to this terrible place? It has no grain or figs, grapevines, or pomegranates. And there is no water to drink!" The Lord said to Moses, "Take the staff, and you and your brother Aaron gather the assembly together. Speak to that rock before their eyes, and it will pour out its water. You will bring water out of the rock for the community so they and their livestock can drink." So, Moses took the staff from the Lord's presence, just as he commanded him. He and Aaron gathered the assembly together in front of the rock, and Moses said to them, "Listen, you rebels, must we bring you water out of this rock?" Then Moses raised his arm and struck the rock twice with his staff. Water gushed out, and the community and their livestock drank.

Numbers 20:2-5, 7-11 (NIV)

Because the emotional upheaval of people in the pews will trigger you as you seek to guide your church through a season of transition, you must determine the story that is driving you. Moses' driving story was striking for liberation. Under stress, he struck out with a liberating force a couple of times: once when striking an Egyptian taskmaster with deadly force, and another time by striking the rock to produce water. In both instances, Moses chose "hitting" instead of "speaking," and both had dire consequences that drove him to live and be condemned to die in the wilderness.

WHAT IS THE STORY DRIVING YOU?

"Hitting" instead of "speaking" is a fitting description for the emotional process that occurs when we are guiding others through the transition process. In most cases, the "hitting" will manifest itself as angry outbursts of denial, fear, blaming, and complaining. Following the stages of grief, it will take some time for the hitting to subside so that speaking can happen.[23] For the past several months, I have spent a lot of time walking pastors, friends, and church leaders through the hitting and speaking processes of change and transition. It has taken me some time to get a handle on a process, and it is still a work in progress (as you too will discover in your journey on the discipleship path). I have made some missteps along the way, but I have come to realize the importance of going slow to go fast[24] when guiding a congregation through the wilderness.

Sounds simple enough, right? But it is not. It ranks as number three on "the hardest thing that I have ever had to do" list, right behind two kidney transplants, and a failed attempt at starting a new church from the ground up. I will discuss the new church start in more detail in the next chapter, but for now, I will focus on the heightened feelings that many of us encounter when we experience any disruptive change.

Most, if not all, of our feelings constellate around three common themes: loss of control, interruption of power, and fear of failure. Admittedly, I was not surprised by how the congregations responded in three predictable ways. What I did not anticipate, however, was how my feelings of "hitting" instead of "speaking" were triggered by what I was experiencing. Unable to name the source of these unwanted feelings, I needed to learn more about the emotional responses during transitions. My quest led me to enroll in a year-long certification program that focused on guiding people and congregations through the transition process, taught by an organization called Liminal Space outside of Seattle, WA. The training program helped me to find the language to unearth my wilderness feelings of loss of control, interruption of power, and fear of failure that have been in opposition to the change that I was trying to help navigate.

---

[23] Elizabeth Kübler-Ross identifies five stages of grief that is equivalent to the hitting stages of transitions: Denial, Anger, Bargaining, Depression and Acceptance. People who are grieving do not necessarily go through the stages in the same order or experience all of them. See Elisabeth Kübler-Ross, M.D. & David Kessler, *On Grief and Grieving: Finding the Meaning of Grief Through the Five Stages of Loss* (New York: Scribner, 2005).

[24] "Go slow to go fast" is a borrowed concept used by CEOs from the business world. See Regan Bach, "Go Slow...To Go Fast!" December 5, 2017, accessed November 20, 2019. https://medium.com/@ reganbach/go-slow-to-go-fast-8c3055e723ed.

THE OPERATIVE NARRATIVE

In my role as District Superintendent, I care deeply about the congregations I work with and desperately want to support their efforts to be healthy and vital. It was sobering to discover that unknowingly lurking underneath my behavior and desire to support churches is what Ron and Jon from Liminal Space call an "operative narrative." This unconscious story operates like a continuously playing, metaphorical scratched CD that starts over and over and represents the story that drives me. Like most operative narratives, our stories develop in childhood. Allow me to share an episode from my father's life to demonstrate how operative narratives originate and can hold a significant influence over our lives.

Daddy was twelve minutes younger than his twin sister. His father was a sharecropper, and as the story goes, when the landowner could no longer make money on cotton in Georgia, my family moved with the lease owner to the Tar Heel state to pick tobacco. Being the third sibling out of four, and the second male, Daddy was in the shadow of his brother, with whom he had a strained relationship. He had to hide his only pair of overalls and tube socks so that his brother would not steal them. Apparently, his efforts to thwart his brother's thievery, and coming of age during the Great Depression (he was born in 1930), turned him into a hoarder. To Daddy, we could never have enough of anything. Our basement felt more like a mini-Sam's Club than a home because we always had shelves full of toilet paper, mouthwash, deodorant, and soft drinks.

When Daddy died, I would find years' worth of unworn ties and unopened shirts that I bought him for Father's Day and Christmas. For him and for many of his Korean War comrades, resources were always scarce, and they were afraid of not having enough to fill their wants and needs. This fear isolated him, and he became a loner.

Like many young boys during this time, he found solace in the Saturday matinee Western cliffhangers. In fact, it was not until I was eight years old that I discovered that Daddy was not a cowboy! After all, he could spin his Colt 45s as if he lived in the Old West. The operative narrative of the hoarder who never had enough influenced the rest of my Daddy's life. And thanks to my Daddy's operative narrative, I was prepared for Y2K with an abundance of supplies some twenty years before it was a thing!

My father's experience is not an isolated one, and you too have wounds that form an operative narrative. The power that these operative narratives hold over you is equivalent to the submerged beliefs of a congregation. Both hold enormous energy and influence on our individual and collective behavior. I will discuss the effects of two churches submerged beliefs in more detail in Chapters 5 and 6.

As insignificant as a brother stealing his younger brother's clothes may seem, this story like many others, has profound impact. Authors Gary McIntosh and Samuel Rima take a slightly different approach in describing an operative narrative as overcoming the dark side. Acknowledging the somewhat sinister tone, and with perhaps even a nod to the Star Wars franchise, they suggest that the dark side or operative narrative is a natural result of human development. They argue that the dark side,

> ...the inner urges, compulsions, and dysfunctions of our personality often go unexamined or remain unknown to us until we experience an emotional explosion. Because it is a part of our nature, we have labeled it the dark side of our personality. However, in spite of the foreboding mental image, [sic] the term dark side creates, it is not, as we shall see, exclusively a negative force in our lives. In almost every case, the factors that eventually undermine us are shadows of the ones that contribute to our success.[25]

As the name "dark side" suggests, there is a negative impact from my operative narrative. And when I am honest with myself, there are also times where I am triggered by my operative narrative and feel judged for my performance or lack thereof, and for not knowing what I am supposed to know. Like the experiences of other pastors, being the so-called expert also impacts my ability to ask for help or to put words to feelings, needs, and desires with those around me. A pastor's ability to guide a church through transitional change largely depends on his or her own ability to change; a leader must first lead one's self before he or she can influence others. As I discovered in both the certification program and coaching cohort, this change begins with identifying and rewriting those operative narratives which are always playing just below the surface of our awareness.[26]

---

[25] Gary L. McIntosh and Samuel D. Rima, Overcoming *The Dark Side of Leadership: How to Become an Effective Leader by Confronting Potential Failures* (Grand Rapids: Baker Books, 2007), 28.

[26] For a summary on practices on how pastors can lead themselves, others, and an organization such as the church, see Beverly A. Thompson and George B. Thompson, Jr., *Ready to Lead: Harnessing the Energy in You and Around You* (Eugene: Wipf & Stock, 2015), Chapter 7.

In like manner, lasting personal change that creates change in the church requires us to face the outdated and scratched CDs playing in our heads. And most of the time, these CDs lead us to exasperating confessions that sound like, "Why do I keep doing that?" Guiding churches through transition and change is hard work, and it will reveal some forgotten and painful stories. Revising your operative narrative will require creating space for God's grace to process the influences behind the tales so that you will be able to guide your congregation through the transition process.

THE GRACE MARGIN

Author and pastor Eric Law describes a process that he calls grace margin[27] to foster group participation during a transition where every person's story and voice is heard, honored, and valued. From Law's work in trying to create a church community where everyone can contribute, he sought to find a way for the voices to be heard. He imposed certain practices so that everyone was given the opportunity and space to share his or her thoughts.

The grace margin is the space where congregations can create between the "safe zone" and the "fear zone." The safe zone is what is familiar. In this safe space, people will reinforce their previously held ideas and old practices. A safe zone is needed. On the flip-side, the fear zone is where people go when they are pushed too far beyond their comfort level. In the fear zone, people tend to lash out and respond to the challenge in hostile and legalistic ways. The unconscious goal in the fear zone is to get back to safety as quickly as possible.

Law argues that creative or adaptive solutions during a transition cannot happen in either the safe zone or the fear zone. One reinforces currently held habits, and the other is so uncomfortable that people shut down. The *grace margin* is akin to what organizational consultant William Bridges calls the neutral zone, the middle phase of the transition process. [28] The grace margin, or neutral zone, is the area in between safety

---

[27] See Eric H. Law, Inclusion: *Making Room for Grace* (Danvers: Chalice Press, 2000), Chapter 7.

[28] See William Bridges, *Transitions: Making Sense of Life's Changes* (Cambridge: Perseus Books Publishing, 1980), Chapter 5.

and fear that can provide your church a time-out to let go of its entrenched ways. Being in the grace margin creates enough "elbow room" to listen to the ignored stories and voices in your congregation and consider genuinely different options without falling into chaos.

WALKING THROUGH LIMINAL SPACES

For our work together, the neutral zone/grace margin represents a liminal space, the threshold between the safe and fear zones where we *discern, dream,* and *develop* paths for a new life. As a spiritual metaphor, a liminal season is a wilderness season where we are broken and reformed. These spaces are also where God's greatest work occurs and are essential to the church's discipleship path.[29]

Guiding congregations on the discipleship path is the process of walking with people through liminal spaces. In these grace margin spaces, people are the most teachable, most willing to let go of the good to take hold of the better, and most willing to risk a loss to gain Christ. To be disciples, we must embrace the in-between and not-yet-formed neutral zone parts of our personhood. Walking through the wilderness together creates a sense of community in the grace margin. The grace margin will help you in the process of guiding your congregation through the grief process of loss. The grace margin creates psychological safety when you are clearing and walking a discipleship path. You can create psychological safety when your team leaders respond with curiosity, intrigue, patience, and genuine interest in thoughts, ideas, stories, and actions that are different from other members of the team and the congregation.[30]

Creating a neutral zone/grace margin will also provide your team with a process to gently hold and honor the sacredness of your personal and congregational stories. The grace margin allows you to listen for understanding instead of needing to be the expert (to be "right" or telling others they are "wrong"). It also allows you to *discern* and *dream* options and goals without fearing criticism or harm. As you will see in

---

[29] For a concise summary on liminality and how it affects congregational change and the revitalization process, see Susan Beaumont, *How to Lead When You Don't Know Where You're Going* (Lanham: Rowman & Littlefield Publishers, 2019) Kindle Edition Chapter 1.

[30] Josh Epperson, "Team Meetings That Create Trust," accessed October 16, 2019. http://www.navalent.com.

the upcoming chapters, your primary role as a guide in creating a neutral zone/grace margin is to:

- Honor the past by listening to the congregation's stories.

- Assess the strengths of the congregation's present.

- Assure the people in the pews of what will remain the same.

- Help people deal with loss, including loss of identity and status.

- Prayerfully help the congregation to imagine God's desired future picture for the church.

CHOOSING YOUR TEAM

So far, we discussed several concepts to help you guide your team. Now, I will shift to providing you with useful tips on how to go about the guiding process. As you select your team, I encourage you to spend time evaluating the people in your church. Primarily, you will be looking for people in your congregation who love your congregation and who are willing to spend a season of wandering to *discern, dream,* and *develop* a discipleship path. After you have determined who fits the criteria:

- Select a team of twelve laypeople plus the pastor, of whom four should be official leaders in your church. (For smaller congregations, I suggest choosing four to six laypeople, of whom three should be official leaders). For example, you should consider anyone who is a chair or team leader to serve on this team.

- In addition to formal leaders, your team should also include four unofficial leaders. You will recognize an unofficial leader as any person who no longer holds official rank or title but holds tremendous influence in your congregation. These informal leaders are the people that the congregation looks to for approval or disapproval of any new venture.

- Finally, your team needs to have four laypeople who are not involved in the day-to-day decision-making processes of the church but attend faithfully.

In this group, I strongly encourage you to select one person under forty and one adolescent. These twelve individuals will make up your 3D Design Team, the people who will help *discern, dream,* and *develop* your church's discipleship path.

The 3D Design Team will spend three months walking the discipleship path of your church through the process of discerning its past success stories, dreaming of a *God-dream* for your church's future, and developing a plan of action and practices to help people walk your discipleship path. At each interval, your team will create focus groups of individuals in your congregation to engage their participation and buy-in. The engagement process, as we will discuss further, will include a couple of information-only town hall meetings in the congregation. Your team will spend the following six months implementing the discipleship path, for a total of nine months. In the next chapter, we will build upon the guiding process and explore how your team might engage with their community.

GROUP SPIRITUAL PRACTICE

In this chapter, I focused on the importance of creating a grace margin[31] to help guide your church through transitions. In this spiritual practice, we will use a grace margin exercise to focus on what it means for your congregation to navigate a transition.

With your selected team of twelve people, begin by centering yourselves, taking a few deep breaths. With eyes closed, sit in silence for a few moments as you prepare to hear the story. After a few moments, your guide will begin to read aloud Exodus 14:10-12, 19-22 aloud. You may want to grab your Bible or read the following in the Common English Bible translation.

> **As Pharaoh approached, the Israelites looked up, and there were the Egyptians, marching after them. They were terrified and cried out to the Lord. They said to Moses, "Was it because there were no graves in Egypt that you brought us to the desert to die? What have you done to us by bringing us out of Egypt? Didn't we say to you in Egypt, 'Leave us alone; let us serve the Egyptians'? It would have been better for us to serve the Egyptians than to die in the desert!"**
>
> **Exodus 14:10**

> **Then the angel of God, who had been traveling in front of Israel's army, withdrew and went behind them. The pillar of cloud also moved from in front and stood behind them, coming between the armies of Egypt and Israel. Throughout the night the cloud brought darkness to the one side and light to the other side; so neither went near the other all night long.[21] Then Moses stretched out his hand over the sea, and all that night**

---

[31] The spiritual practices in this book are borrowed with permission from Beverly and George Thompson's grace margin exercises, which they adapted from Eric Law's work on mutual invitation. See Beverly A. George B. Thompson, Jr., *Grace for the Journey: Practices and Possibilities for In-Between Times* (Herndon: The Alban Institute, 2011). Kindle Edition; and Eric H. Law, *The Wolf Shall Dwell with the Lamb: A Spirituality for Leadership in a Multicultural Community* (St. Louis: Chalice Press, 1993), Chapter 9.

the Lord drove the sea back with a strong east wind and turned it into dry land. The waters were divided,[22] and the Israelites went through the sea on dry ground, with a wall of water on their right and on their left.

Exodus 14:19

Once the text has been read, ask participants to sit quietly with what they have heard for a few moments. After a time of silent prayer, invite participants to reflect on the following questions:

1. As an individual, where do you go when you are confused or upset?

2. What does your congregation do when it is faced with upsetting or confusing news?

3. Using the metaphor of facing obstacles in front and behind, how might your congregation move forward anyway?

4. What will you do when God calls you to enter into the sea that hasn't parted yet?

Sit with these offerings for a few quiet moments. Now, begin to imagine what your church might experience if God is leading you through your figurative Red Sea today.

After the first question has been asked, sit in silence for ten seconds. If persons choose not to accept the invitation to share at this time and prefer to pass, that is their choice, and it is okay. The person who passes still invites another person, by name, to share. In this way, no one feels excluded even if he/she chooses not to speak. Value each reflection with gratitude, without judgment or agreement.

Remember to honor the ten seconds of silence following each reflection. After each person has had the opportunity to share, you may ask for clarification from one another and begin to dialogue about God's grace-filled possibilities. Repeat this process for the second question. This process can take up to fifteen minutes depending on how many people choose to speak. Of course, some will share longer, and some will not share at all. Close your time together with your sentence prayers of praise and thanksgiving. Please allow 20-30 minutes for this portion of the exercise.

3

ENGAGEMENT

Asking About Life

After this the Lord appointed seventy-two others and sent them two by two ahead of him to every town and place where he was about to go.

Luke 10:1 (NIV)

If you want your church to grow, stop trying to attract people. Start trying to engage people.[32]

Carey Nieuwhof

People are not looking for a church. People are looking for community and engagement. This news was the painful lesson I learned as a failed church planter a few years ago. It took me a long time to come to terms with my failure. After all, I sincerely believed that God called me to

---

[32] Carey Nieuwhof, "5 Reasons Why Engagement is the New Church Attendance," accessed October 12, 2019. https://careynieuwhof.com/5-reasons-why-engagement-is-the-new-church-attendance/.

plant a new church. My thoughts were, if God called me, then God would also equip me for the work. With this assurance, I left my position as a college vice-president and leaped with faith to start a church from scratch. I placed all of my "eggs in this one basket." I believed that I was carrying an Easter basket that promised opportunities for hope and new life. Little did I realize that carrying this basket also meant that I would encounter all of the elements of Easter: a Good Friday death blow, and a Holy Saturday of trying to figure out where I went wrong before I could experience Easter.

As a planter-to-be, I attended church planter boot camp, was assigned a coach, and worked alongside a successful church planter at a growing church. From all accounts, I had all of the support (both financial and human) and training that I needed to begin a church. And like most church planters, I had a lofty vision of what the new church could be. I also had a healthy dose of strategy and the understanding of the system necessary to birth something new. But having those tools in my tool kit was not very useful for the relational work of connecting with people in the community, including with my new team.

As I began to recruit a launch team, the individuals who would commit to helping me start the church, I discovered how difficult it was to make the shift from making members to making disciples. I recruited those who were no longer actively attending church as the people on the team, and they only saw the church, not the community around the church where we were to plant the new church.

SHIFTING FROM INSIDE TO OUT

In a short time, my launch team quickly discovered that planting a church is not the same as attending an established church. Instead, it requires shifting from insider thinking to thinking outside the box to engage people in the community. This shift was our most difficult challenge. Unfortunately, the team that I gathered around me could not make the shift, and I lacked the tools to train them.

At the time, I wished someone had told me that the best path forward for churches, especially new church starts, is a return to the leaders' foundational practices. I now know that the best path is less about reinventing the wheel and more about remembering the histories and building on the founding principles from the church's origin.[33]

The shift sounds like the standard operating procedure for all chur̄ Wrong! As simple as these shifts may appear on paper, they prove to be painfully awkward. This truth was especially real for my launch team anū church plant. I eventually pulled the plug for not being able to make this shift in an acceptable time frame.[34]

For long-time established churches, which likely may describe your church, the process is slightly different from a new church start, but the results are the same: Engagement outside the church walls involves exercising our atrophied muscles to push away from our comfort zones. With proper diet and regular exercise, our churches can repair their muscles to do the heavy lifting of intentionally engaging their communities by facing continued uncertainty.

At times, the process may feel a lot like trying to turn a big ship moving at full speed on a dime. It will take several miles of travel to change the momentum of the vessel and to begin to turn the ship. Similarly, it will take significant time and energy from the congregation working together with the Holy Spirit to turn the church. But it can be done!

COMMUNITY ENGAGEMENT

Community engagement is about mission, and mission is about being sent. Abraham was sent. Moses was sent. Jesus was sent. Being "sent" requires that we are going places and doing things. When Jesus called the disciples, they had to rearrange their lives. They had to put down their nets, follow Jesus, and then be sent out, doing things they had never done before. In the same way, Jesus wants to send our members inside the church outside into the community. Australian author and missional strategist Alan Hirsch provides a working definition of what it means to engage people inside the church to enhance engagement outside the church walls. In describing the creation of a community to explore a common mission, he explains:

---

[33] Phil Maynard, *Membership to Discipleship: Growing Mature Disciples Who Make Disciples* (Excellence in Ministry and Coaching, 2015), 28-31.

[34] For more on what I learned from this experience, see Quincy Brown, "Failure in Church Planting Is an Option," May 17, 2016. https://seedbed.com/failure-in-church-planting-is-an-option/.

'nvolves adventure and movement, and it describes
'erience of togetherness that only really happens
' people inspired by the vision of a better world
 ⸌mpt to do something about it.[35]

⸌ɪ's comments provide the foundation for the church to gather
⸌ɔund a common mission of making disciples inside the church walls
to make disciples outside the church walls through engagement. Using
Hirsch's notion of engagement to make a better world, I have created a
community engagement questionnaire to help you listen to the stories that
are being told outside your walls. Here are the questions.[36]

Community Engagement Questions

1. How long have you lived in this community?

2. What do you think is the greatest need in this community?

3. What are your hopes and dreams for your family?

4. What advice can you give a church on how to provide hope to
    help families deal with their life struggles?

5. Who do you know in your community who has the skills for
    helping to provide hope?

6. How can we pray for you?

---

[35] Alan Hirsch, *The Forgotten Ways: Reactivating the Missional Church* (Grand Rapids: Baker Publishing Group, 2006, Kindle Edition, 221.

[36] The Community Engagement Questionnaire found in the appendix was created in partnership with Liminal Space Board Chairman Ron Carucci and Executive Director Jonathan DeWaal. http://www.inaliminalspace.org. The questionnaire used by permission was part of my initial work in the Liminal Space cohort. See appendix for the full survey.

Using appreciative inquiry, a process that focuses on what is working well and why, and the assessment questions for community engagement, your church can discover the emotional needs of your community. Ron Carucci points to this critical knowledge when discussing the practices of entrepreneurial startups that can apply to churches. In an article written for *Forbes Magazine* that highlights the success of a successful upstart company, he argues,

> **Every entrepreneur dreams of creating something of enduring impact – something that truly inspires change in their industry, in society, around the globe. In my experience with entrepreneurs, they often misunderstand the value they are offering to the market – the problem they are solving, the need they are meeting. They see the world from their idea out and dangerously fall in love with what they believe makes their product or service amazing. But great startups work from the market back, listening to the unmet needs and pains of those they want to serve, and position themselves accordingly.**[37]

Since entrepreneur startups are outside your church walls and are trying to reach the same people, your church can learn from their entrepreneurial methods to help you with community engagement. The assessment encourages you to identify places of business within a two mile radius of your church (some areas may require longer distances) and ask the managers these questions. As you begin the engagement work, please do not ask the customers. Your only agenda is to listen to the stories that people give you and NOT to invite people to your church. You may invite others at a later time in the process. At least for now, you are seeking information and help from the community. You do not want the community to know of your church as only being interested in inviting people to join the church without concern about the individual's or community's needs!

To avoid proselytizing, I encourage you to ask the same questions to the guests who attend your existing community events on your church

---

[37] Ron Carucci, "The Secret Ingredients Behind Impossible Burger's Runaway Success," August 26, 2019. https://www.forbes.com/sites/roncarucci/2019/08/26/the-secret-ingredients-behind-impossible-burgers-runaway-success/#7d08606a4f42.

grounds, such as trunk or treat or fall festivals, Easter egg hunts, blessing of the animals, back to school events, and so on. After your team has gathered and sorted the data from both exercises, watch for themes to emerge. For instance, an issue of low high school graduation rates might arise. Food insecurity might be another theme to emerge. The list of concerns is endless, but to determine whether the problems are opportunities for your church, you must assess whether each idea fits with your church's *God-dream*. (We will discuss your vision in further detail in Chapter 7.) By using this asset mapping exercise, I am making a fundamental assumption that the resources are "out there" – outside the walls and *not* "in here" – inside the walls of your congregation. In many cases, however, these resources are often missed and may not be recognized until there is an intentional process of gathering a team together to begin to identify them. As you gather your team to begin the assessment process for engagement, here is the question that guides your engagement work:

- **Are there resources available to address the need?**

Addressing this question will help you make an important step in being prepared to move forward with a new ministry. Responding to this question will also help you to determine whether the way you do church is relevant for the people in your immediate context. Likely, people outside your church (and yes, quite a few insiders, too) feel confused and overwhelmed in a changing world that is increasingly noisy and busy.

THE GOOD NEWS IS THAT THERE IS AN OVERARCHING THEME TO WHAT PEOPLE OUTSIDE THE CHURCH ARE SEEKING. PEOPLE ARE LOOKING FOR LIFE: WHAT IT IS AND HOW THEY CAN FIND IT.

Upon completing the assessment, I anticipate that you will find that people are asking questions about life. It is not that people's questions mean that justification and forgiveness of sins are no longer critical. Instead, people are not versed in these issues and are not interested until your church can answer the question: What's in it for me (WIIFM)?

Sounding more like radio call letters, WIIFM is what Roger Dean Duncan[38] suggests that people tune in to when working through transitions and change. Duncan argues that WIIFM does not imply that most people are selfish. Instead, he affirms the "me" in his argument focuses on the personal context. Duncan's insights on the context during change prompts me to ask you a discernment question: "What questions are the people outside your church asking?" One thing is sure: People outside your church are not asking about how they can join your church. Listening to the stories you hear from inside and outside your church walls will help you discern a path to address the shifts to connect with people and offer solutions to their problems.

In this chapter, we have spent time reviewing the concept of discipleship. In the process, we learned the need to determine what is going inside and outside the church's walls. My hope is that you become part of people's lives and share God's love in tangible ways. In the next chapter, we will delve further into the theories that support the *discerning* process. Your church will begin to discern your path by exploring a small rural congregation and its quest to increase worship attendance.

INDIVIDUAL QUESTIONS FOR REFLECTION

1. As you think about the area surrounding your church, what do you think is the greatest need in your community?

---

[38] Roger Dean Duncan, "In Times of Change, 'What's In It for Me?' Is the Question You Need to Answer," September 14, 2012, accessed on August 21, 2019. https://www.fastcompany.com/3001250/times-change-whats-it-me-question-you-need-answer/.

2. As you think about the people living in a three mile radius of your church, what do you believe are the hopes and dreams of their families?

3. What advice do you think people outside the walls of your church will provide on how to provide hope to help families deal with today's pressures?

After you have addressed these questions individually, as we discussed earlier in the chapter, I encourage you to pair together in twos and use the Community Assessment Questionnaire found in Appendix C to ask people who attend your outreach programs and places in your community.

4

TRADITIONS

What Questions Are You Trying to Answer?

When Joseph arrived at Shechem, a man found him wandering around in the fields and asked him, "What are you looking for?"

Genesis 37:14b-15 (NIV)

Questions are taken for granted rather than given a starring role in the human drama. All my teaching and consulting experience has taught me that what builds a relationship, what solves problems, what moves things forward is asking the right questions.[39]

Edgar Schein

How do we get people to come to our church? This was the exasperating question that Mr. Benny, an 84-year-old widowed and lifelong member of Mt. Sinai Church, kept asking.

Mr. Benny lamented: "It's a shame that young people today don't attend church the way we used to." Getting more adamant and animated, he erupted into a sermonic monologue of "the good old days" of when he was

---

[39] Edgar H. Schein, *Humble Inquiry: The Gentle Art of Asking Instead of Telling* (San Francisco: Berrett-Koehler Publishers, Inc., 2013), 3.

young, and he got "saved" at a Wednesday night camp meeting service. He recounted the many revivals, camp meetings, church anniversaries, and homecoming services that he and his peers attended. As he was talking, I noticed several Mt. Sinai members nodding in approval for his nostalgic retelling of the church's past.

During a break in the training, I learned that Mr. Benny's life rotates around his immediate and extended family, his small tight-knit rural community, and, of course, Mt. Sinai. I asked him to share why he loved his church so much. Mr. Benny responded, "We are the little church with a big heart! We are a small and welcoming church." I asked him to share a story of when he felt Mt. Sinai was at its most welcoming. He quickly recounted,

We used to bake fresh bread for new families who moved to town. Church members divided into groups of twos and made house calls to new families to let them know about our church. We wanted our new neighbors to know that in our church, we take a personal approach to connect with people.

After asking Mr. Benny to tell stories about his tight-knit community, other church leaders began to imitate him and share their stories. A significant number of stories recalled memories of how the town used to thrive on local manufacturing, but times had changed. The two large factories on the outskirts of the city closed. The new hospital relocated to the next county, the economy was declining, and people were scrambling to find second jobs to offset their low-paying main ones. Despite the real struggle to find meaningful work, Mt. Sinai's members were proud of their hard-working community and small church.

My experience with Mr. Benny has become commonplace with churches across the country. Due to no fault of their own, the communities outside their churches have changed. The struggle for churches like Mt. Sinai is they do not know how to adjust to those outside changes. The church continued to ask, "How do we get a newer and younger audience in our pews on Sunday?" When well-meaning church members like Mr. Benny seek silver bullet answers,[40] they want someone to give a clear, ready-made, and cure-all answer. For some, it is the answer

---

[40] Daniel Im, *No Silver Bullets: 5 Small Shifts That Will Transform Your Ministry* (Nashville: B&H Publishing Group, 2017), 155.

to the question: "How do we get new people into the church who will honor our traditions?" Others seek answers to, "How do we address our shrinking congregation that has either plateaued or is in decline?" Still, others want to know, "How will we survive if we do not have the annual fundraiser?" And then, a large percentage of churches have never considered the questions they are trying to answer. Frankly, it is possible to engage in the top five or seven practices to turn your church around that may produce results. But in every case, the results will always be short-lived because the quick-fix approach does not address the church culture.

TRADITIONS AND NOSTALGIA

As you seek to address the quick fix questions, the odds are good that your answers will hint at outcomes that you would like your church to produce. Without finding a silver bullet answer, many churches will cling to nostalgia and tradition. Like tradition, nostalgia is not easy to overcome. Instead, it provides an insight into the church's past stories.

NOSTALGIA IS THE RESIDUE FROM A CHURCH'S PAST SUCCESSES THAT NO LONGER WORK TODAY.

Gil Rendle argues that nostalgia is the path that leads people away from what is currently bothering them towards an earlier time and missing of the past. It echoes my experience with Mt. Sinai by representing the path to the "warmly remembered past." In simple terms, nostalgia connects people to a former time that was perceived to be better than it is now.[41]

It was abundantly clear that nostalgia was what Mr. Benny was referring to as the "good old days." When hearing his stories, I made the mistake that many pastors make: I insisted that their tradition was something to overcome. Being misguided, I advised how to move the debris to clear a new path, but at every turn, I encountered resistance. The more I gave statistics, best practices, and opportunities for growth, the more the leaders from Mt. Sinai dug in their heels about their past. It felt like insanity—both

---

[41] Gil Rendle. *Quietly Courageous: Leading the Church in a Changing World* (Lanham: Rowman & Littlefield Publishing Group, Inc., 2019), 155-156.

the leaders and I were continuing to do the same things but we expected different results! It is enough to say that I felt frustrated, and the leaders were disappointed that I could not provide immediate answers.

DISAPPOINTMENT AND FRUSTRATION HAPPEN WHEN CHURCHES CANNOT DETACH THEMSELVES FROM THEIR TRADITIONS.

George B. Thompson, Jr., proposes that tradition or nostalgia is not bad in itself.[42] Unknowingly, my actions exposed my bias against their traditions and the gaps between where Mt. Sinai used to be and where they need to go for survival. Fortunately, the conversations did not turn into arguments ending in stalemates and hurt feelings.

After the training, I reflected on what went wrong at Mt. Sinai and what I could have done differently. Like the overgrowth and weeds on our neighborhood path that blocked a way forward, I was so bogged down by my bias that I was unable to embrace a spirit of curiosity. Instead of being the expert who told them what to do, I needed to seek other ways forward by asking about their stories.

ASKING INSTEAD OF TELLING

There is a difference between telling the answer and asking questions. Edgar Schein's work on "humble inquiry" argues that telling people the answer is how most of us have been taught to respond to a challenge or problem.[43] As experts, we are supposed to have the information and knowledge to solve any question or concern. But without building trusting relationships, our experience can feel like fallen debris blocking a path forward.

When I first visited Mt. Sinai, the members asked me the following "closed-ended" question: "Don't you just love our church?" This question required me to give a "yes" or "no" response but did not allow room for much else. I nodded in compliance, wanting to make an excellent first impression. I thought that an "open-ended" and appreciative question

---

[42] George B. Thompson, Jr., *Futuring Your Church: Finding Your Vision and Making it Work* (Cleveland: United Church Press, 1999), 16.

[43] Edgar Schein, *Humble Inquiry: The Gentle Art of Asking Instead of Telling* (San Francisco: Berrett-Koehler Publishers, Inc., 2013), 2.

would have been more appropriate to help me build relationships and share meaningful conversations.[44] Here is an example of an open-ended question: "What do you see that is lovely about our church?" Admittedly, I did not expect the members or the pastor to ask this in such a way that would invite me to explore with them. Both types of questions address love for the church. But the latter is framed to receive more information to help Mt. Sinai learn how to improve what I (or others) may not have loved about the church. Of course, a best practice procedure would be to establish a relationship with members before discussing these ideas. Besides providing information on what is not working, open-ended questions can also help to appreciate what your church does well. Cameron Harder's work is instructive on this process. He writes:

Appreciative inquiry builds upon the right questions. The questions look for what works instead of what has gone wrong, for what we value and care about rather than those things we reject, and for what we hope for rather than what we fear.[45]

GROUP SPIRITUAL PRACTICE

Through this spiritual practice, I invite your team to discuss your church's past success stories. As with all of the spiritual practices in this book, your team will need to select a facilitator or guide for the exercise. The guide does not need to be a biblical scholar or hold formal leadership in the church. The only qualification for the guide is reading and following the instructions laid out in the exercise.

Begin by centering yourselves, taking a few deep breaths. With eyes closed, sit in silence for a few moments as you prepare to hear the story. After a few moments, your guide will begin to read aloud Deuteronomy 26:5-9. You may want to grab your Bible or read the following text:

---

[44] Cameron Harder suggests that "appreciative inquiry" questions arise out of faith and look in some way for the affirmative action of God in the world. (See Cameron Harder, *Discovering the Other: Asset-Based Approaches to Building Community Together* (Herndon: Rowman & Littlefield Publishers, 2013), Kindle Edition, Location 378.

[45] Ibid., Location 28005.

...you shall make this response before the Lord your God: "A wandering Aramean was my ancestor; he went down into Egypt and lived there as an alien, few in number, and there he became a great nation, mighty and populous. When the Egyptians treated us harshly and afflicted us, by imposing hard labor on us, we cried to the Lord, the God of our ancestors; the Lord heard our voice and saw our affliction, our toil, and our oppression. The Lord brought us out of Egypt with a mighty hand and an outstretched arm, with a terrifying display of power, and with signs and wonders; and he brought us into this place and gave us this land, a land flowing with milk and honey."

Once the text has been read, sit quietly for a few moments with what you have heard. After a time of meditation, your guide will invite you to reflect on the following questions:

1. As you reflect on your church's history, can you identify moments of nostalgia? In the space below, list those nostalgic times.

2. How can we celebrate the stories of our past and become more responsive to our current context?

3. How is God calling our church into a land flowing with milk and honey, and an opportunity for new life?

4. What would the three wishes you have for your congregation be if you were free to hope for the best?

5. What might you be able to contribute to help one of these wishes come true?

After the first question has been asked, sit in silence for ten seconds. One by one, each person will invite another member of the group by name to share his or her reflections.

Allow ten seconds of silence after each person has spoken before inviting another to share. If someone chooses not to speak, but rather wishes to pass, this is okay. The person who passes still invites another person, by name, to share. Value each reflection with gratitude, without judgment or agreement.

Remember to honor the ten seconds of silence following each reflection. After each person has had the opportunity to share, you may ask for clarification from one another and begin to dialogue about God's grace-filled possibilities. Repeat this process for the second question. Close your time together with your sentence prayers of praise and thanksgiving. Please allow twenty-thirty minutes for this section.

5

DISCERN

Story-Shifts Inside and Outside of Church

Trust in the LORD with all your heart and lean not on your understanding; in all your ways submit to him, and he will make your paths straight.

Proverbs 3:5-6 (NIV)

But to make you understand, to give you my life, I must tell you a story—and there are so many—stories of childhood, stories of school, love, marriage, and death, and so on.[46]

Virginia Woolf

As I discussed in the previous chapter, most of us have not been trained to ask open-ended questions of discernment that invite stories. Mt. Sinai's leadership insisted that I tell them "how" to increase worship attendance without engaging in the *discerning* process. In this chapter, we will discuss the theory behind the first leg of the path: *discern*.

---

[46] Sue Roe and Susan Sellers, eds. *The Cambridge Companion to Virginia Woolf* (Cambridge: Cambridge University Press, 2010), 257.

WHAT IS DISCERNMENT?

In defining what I mean by discerning, the *discern* process means going deeper in conversation to clarify and discover factors and awareness.

THE DISCERN PROCESS TAKES A DEEP DIVE INTO YOUR CHURCH'S PAST SUCCESS STORIES TO APPRECIATE WHAT HAS SHAPED YOUR TRADITIONS AND BEHAVIOR. DISCERN QUESTIONS ARE "WHY" QUESTIONS THAT UNEARTH CORE STORIES OF PROFOUND ENERGY RESIDING JUST BELOW THE SURFACE OF TRADITIONS.

Congregations experience *discernment* as attentiveness to God that, over time, develops into a perception of God's intentional story for the church. *Discernment* calls for a community to help us beyond the personal to see beyond personal feelings to determine what God is doing within the collective whole.[47]

DISCERNMENT REQUIRES US TO LISTEN TO GOD'S SPIRIT TO GUIDE US LIKE A CLOUD AND PILLAR OF FIRE THROUGH OUR MO MBTS OF UNCERTAINTY.[48]

Susan Beaumont provides a starting place in the challenging work required in the *discerning* process. She writes,

> **[To discern] ...requires unknowing, a recognition that we do not have the answers that are needed and that we are willing to remain open to previously unimagined possibilities.**[49]

---

[47] Susan Beaumont, *How to Lead,* 77-78.

[48] In the book of Exodus, God uses the pillar of cloud by day and the support of fire by night to guide the path of the Israelites during their exodus from Egyptian bondage through the wilderness en route to the Promised Land. See Exodus 13:21–22.

[49] Susan Beaumont, "Budget Shortfalls and Discernment," accessed August 30, 2019. http://www.susanbeaumont.com/budget-shortfalls-and-discernment/.

The Bible is chock-full with admonishments of discernment, being still, remaining open, and making our request to God. A couple of the most compelling *discern*ment texts that I frequently hear are:

Be still and know that I am God; I will be exalted among the nations, I will be exalted in the earth."

Psalm 46:10 (NIV)

Dear friends, do not believe every spirit but test the spirits to see whether they are from God because many false prophets have gone out into the world.

1 John 4:11 (NIV)

These texts and others like them provide clear guidance for the *discerning* process. The challenge occurs when the church would rather spend all of its time huddled together in prayer and *not* follow through with the answer that God reveals during the *discerning* process. Prayer for discernment is foundational for your church's discipleship process, but at some point, God will ask you to get up from your knees and follow God's response to your prayers. The problem with the *discerning* process is, of course, when things get tense from an imposing crisis, we do more telling than asking. In your church, you may try to "attract" a younger demographic by adding a contemporary worship experience and telling younger people why they should attend your church. If this is a familiar story for your church, you are not alone. New skills are required to help your church move away from the default of "telling." Specifically, we need to unlearn what we know and re-learn the art of drawing someone in by asking questions to which we do not already know the answer.

Asking such questions will help you build relationships based on curiosity in the other person to *discern* their next steps on the path. Perhaps it is helpful to think of the *discern* process as becoming a freshman in high school or college, moving into a different world, and having to figure out the cultural shifts of new customs, traditions, values, and behaviors. I will illustrate this experience with a story from my freshman year in college.

THE SHIFT KEY

I did not take a typing class in high school. Since I was going into the electronic engineering technology field of study, naively, it never occurred to me that I would need to know how to type. Consequently, I taught myself how to type by observing others. During the first semester of my freshman year, while writing college papers and creating code for BASIC and Pascal programming languages, I mimicked my lab partner, Todd, to discover where to position my fingers on the keyboard.

Todd was farther along than I was, and he was comfortable with computers. I was a novice. By frequently asking him questions and sharing our stories, we became more than lab partners; we became close friends who worked on everything together. Todd taught me about using double spaces after sentences, a practice that has since changed with the advent of texting! He also taught me about the shift key, the key that allowed me to change a lower-case letter to a capital letter and change the number keys to symbols. I discovered that I could increase my typing speed by using the shift key instead of tapping the caps lock key on and off.

The shift key uncovered unseen characters that appeared on the physical key but could not be accessed without the shift key. Using the shift key also serves as a metaphor for the process of addressing change in a church by showing the information not obvious to the casual observer. For churches like Mt. Sinai, metaphorically typing the shift key means beginning the process of *discerning* the story shifts happening behind certain church practices and outside its walls. Such a process is fraught with difficulty as the stories we remember and repeat are celebration stories while we omit stories that stir painful feelings.

DISCERNING STORY SHIFTS

The world changes every seven-to-eight seconds, and the stories told outside the church are rapidly shifting.[50]

STORY SHIFTS ARE ANOTHER WAY OF TALKING ABOUT A PARADIGM SHIFT.

---

[50] Olu Brown, *4D Impact: Smash Barriers Like a Smart Church* (Nashville: Abingdon Press, 2019), 1.

Paradigm shifts—the profoundly significant change that requires rethinking and re-creation of all things—radically challenge our underlying assumptions.[51] An example of a paradigm shift can be the movement away from members to disciples. We will discuss this paradigm shift in more detail in the second half of this book as we focus on walking the path. For now, we will take a look at the origin of what constitutes a paradigm.

First discussed by Thomas Kuhn in his book *The Structure of Scientific Revolutions,*[52] a paradigm is the way we look at the world through a particular set of lenses. Paradigms are the mental framework that help us to interpret the world. In lay terminology, a paradigm is an accepted way that things are done. It follows the axiom, "If it ain't broke, don't fix it."

Most churches are accustomed to a paradigm that Kuhn calls incremental change. For example, a long-standing paradigm in several churches is the frequently used projection for yearly finances in the budgeting process. Church leaders are more than happy to keep the overall budget projections under a cost of living increase while slightly increasing program and ministry funding. Incremental changes represent the norm for churches, but it is the rapid, radical shifts in the culture that trip up most churches. A brief comparison between gradual and radical change is helpful for our conversation.

The Toyota Prius Hybrid car is an example of gradual, incremental change. As different as it was when it arrived on the market, the hybrid car did not change the nature or capability of the automobile. It is still a vehicle with four wheels, seats for passengers, a steering wheel, and all of the bells and whistles of a car. The different or incremental change is that it adds an alternative source of power. Hybrid vehicles have not become the standard for automobiles but merely offer an alternative for environmentally conscious consumers.

The iPhone, by contrast, is an example of a paradigm shift. Before its arrival, mobile phones had buttons a person could press to dial, in much the same way as the touch-dial phones of a previous generation. The iPhone does not have buttons, but rather a touch screen that does not require a stylus. Before the iPhone, "flip phones" and phones with a split

---

[51] Gilbert R. Rendle, *Journey in the Wilderness: New Life for Mainline Churches* (Nashville: Abingdon Press, 2010), Chapter 1.

[52] Thomas Kuhn, *The Structure of Scientific Revolutions* (Chicago: The University of Chicago Press, 1970).

keyboard and screen, were typical. Almost all the phones we carry around in our back pockets today boast full touch-screen capabilities.

As an example of radical change, the iPhone re-imagined the understanding of what a "phone" could do. Using nothing but a person's index finger, as Steve Jobs famously advertised, the iPhone rewrote the rules for many markets, including photography, e-commerce, maps/navigation systems, television, movies, and music. The iPhone also changed the standard for all present smartphones. For many churches, the remedy often sought is to blame the paradigm shifts on the world outside its walls (e.g., cultural changes, demographics, economics, and so on). This cultural shift lies at the heart of the radical changes outside our churches. Perhaps a brief conversation about how the cultural shift can inform your team on what your congregation is experiencing with declining attendance is needed.

CHRISTENDOM'S STORY-SHIFT

Christendom is a word that most people in your church will not recognize. It is a paradigm descriptor for the culture that emerged beginning in 313 A.D. when Emperor Constantine converted to and legalized Christianity. Years later, Roman Emperor Theodosius made Christianity the official religion of the Roman Empire through the Edict of Milan in 380 AD.[53] Former associate editor of *Forbes Magazine*, Alvin Toffler, argues that the "wave" of the Christendom paradigm[54] was dominant in the United States until 1955.

This year marked the first time that the number of white-collar workers outnumbered the blue-collar workers. Blue-collar workers championing manual labor symbolized the best of the Industrial Revolu-

---

[53] Loren B. Mead, *The Once and Future Church: Reinventing the Congregation For a New Mission Frontier* (New York: The Alban Institute, 1993), 187.

[54] Mike Regele argues that Christendom boasted of three pillars of the community: public schools, church, and the family. Each of the components has lost its luster and has taken a significant hit in the broader culture. The loss of prayer in schools, decline in church attendance, and high rates of divorce leading to blending families are some visible effects of the Christendom paradigm shift. See Mike Regele and Mark Schulz, *Death of the Church: The Church Has a Choice: To Die as a Result of its Resistance to Change or to Die in Order to Live* (Grand Rapids: Zondervan Publishing House, 1995).

tion assembly-line work.[55] The shift to the white-collar worker symbolized a move away from industry to information, where work happened in an organizational setting, often away from an assembly line.

For the church, the shift ultimately means that the long era of the Christendom culture is coming to an end. Several authors, including Phyllis Tickle, through her groundbreaking work, *The Great Emergence,*[56] have written extensively about this ending. For our purposes, we will accept that this phenomenon is happening. The church's place in the dominant culture has shifted. The experience is akin to the story that begins the book of Exodus: a king arose who no longer "knew Joseph" (Exodus 1:6-8, NRSV).

The end of the Christendom paradigm is also what unknowingly lies at the heart of the lament behind "everything changed when they took prayer out of school and removed the Ten Commandments out of the courthouses." Susan Beaumont's summary of Diana Butler Bass's work echoes Tickle's thoughts by asserting,

The institutional church is losing its efficacy and its membership. Something in the church needs stripping away so that the church can profoundly reorient itself if it is going to remain relevant in this new world order.[57]

This lament and others like it, such as the loss of traditional values of the nuclear family, acknowledge that something has gone wrong. Regrettably, the dominant explanation for the loss makes the culture the enemy without going beyond the pain point to the symptom of the paradigm shifting.

---

[55] Alvin Toffler, *The Third Wave* (New York: Bantam Books, 1981), 14.

[56] See Phyllis Tickle, *The Great Emergence: How Christianity is Changing and Why* (Grand Rapids: Baker Books, 2008).

[57] Susan Beaumont, *How to Lead,* 17.

IT IS IMPORTANT TO NOTE THAT THE CULTURAL ASSUMPTIONS AND VALUES OUTSIDE THE WALLS OF THE CHURCH ARE COMING TO AN END, BUT NOT THE CHURCH ITSELF.

On the contrary, the church, the called-out ones for Christian assembly, the people who follow Jesus, will continue to stand.

In Matthew's Gospel, Jesus says it best:

This is the rock on which I will put together my church, a church so expansive with energy that not even the gates of hell will be able to keep it out.

Matthew 16:18 (MSG)

In this era of the post-Christendom story shift, the stories for the future are yet to be determined. It is noteworthy to mention that uncertainty causes some churches to remain stuck indefinitely in the *discern* phase of seeking God's will on what to do next. They do not want to address the story shift since they see change itself as the problem.

Discerning a paradigm shift is not as hard as it sounds. You can probably identify several paradigm shifts in your city. You might not call it a paradigm shift, but the effect is similar to what Dorothy Gale in *The Wizard of Oz* once famously said: "Toto, I have a feeling that we're not in Kansas anymore."

DISCERNING YOUR PARADIGM SHIFT STARTS WITH TAKING A DEEP DIVE INTO YOUR PAST STORIES TO IDENTIFY WHERE GOD'S POWER WAS ACTIVE IN THE LIFE OF YOUR CONGREGATION.

MEMBERSHIP HAS PRIVILEGES

As we discovered from my early experience with Mr. Benny at Mt. Sinai, reviewing the stories of the past may reveal haunting ghost stories that hold your church hostage. The *discern* process will also expose submerged beliefs that are fueling your church's energy. In Mt. Sinai's case, it felt like the power and privilege of membership were places of high strength.

Well before the current members of Mr. Benny's time, the church's culture championed the privileges of being a church member. For Mr. Benny and his contemporaries, one of the principal rights was having a vote. Because of this, most of Mr. Benny's time in the church was served in making decisions. Any attempt at *discerning* why Mt. Sinai did what it did was shut down in favor of quickly deciding on what to do next. It was uncomfortable for Mr. Benny and his peers to sort through the church's stories that focused on decision-making to determine the values and submerged beliefs which fueled so much its desperation behavior.

Many churches share a similar history of equating their role as church leaders as making decisions instead of making disciples. Richard Rohr offers a helpful distinction between *discernment* and decision-making:

> **Discernment is not the same as decision-making. Reaching a decision can be a straightforward process:**
>
> • **We can consider our goals and options.**
>
> • **We can list the pros and cons of each possible choice.**
>
> • **We choose the action that meets our goal most effectively.**

Unlike decision-making, *discernment* is about listening and responding to that place within our souls, where our deepest desires align with God's desire.[58]

DISCERNMENT IS NOT DECISION-MAKING. DISCERNMENT FOCUSES ON GOD'S PURPOSE FOR PEOPLE INSIDE AND OUTSIDE THE CHURCH WALLS.

Decision-making in many churches will lead to meeting personal preferences, but *discernment* leads to a relative path of engagement with the gospel by people seeking something more in life. Your church must stop focusing on decision-making that is exclusively for members. You must shift the emphasis to capture the hearts of people with an excellent vision to meet real needs that translate into changed lives.

---

[58] Richard Rohr, "Discernment versus Decision-Making," Center for Action and Contemplation, May 28, 2018, accessed August 22, 2019. https://cac.org/discernment-versus-decision-making-2018-05-31/.

INDIVIDUAL QUESTIONS FOR REFLECTION

Cameron Harder urges that if your church takes life outside your walls seriously, you can offer your community the gift of discovering the other. He provides three questions as a guide to help your church see itself and the other. Regrettably, I was unaware of these questions when working with Mt. Sinai Church, but I offer them to you as a new tool to begin the conversation with your church.

1. Are there memorable stories of your past that your church continues to celebrate? If so, list them below.

2. What are the stories of the past that your congregation omits? List them below and discern why you think they have been omitted?

3. As you think about your church's context, can you identify the post-Christendom shifts in your community? List your responses below.

I encourage you to spend time with these questions in your congregation and listen to stories so that a clear path emerges. You may not like the path that you are on or the stories you hear, but to navigate your way to creating a new path, you will need to pay closer attention to discoveries which emerge from these questions. Helping Mt. Sinai required me to use appreciative inquiry to rediscover and reclaim their mission: to make disciples that form communities by connecting with and imitating Jesus.

6

CHANGES

Not Like It Used to Be

But how could we possibly sing the LORD's song on foreign soil?

Psalms 137:4 (CEB)

I think fear is probably the largest inhibitor of this kind of change. It's hard to move forward when churches, pastors, and committees are terrified that if they change something their biggest givers will leave the church. Jesus is calling the church into change, and the church says, 'We have to check the budget first.' And I get it. But really church people need to be braver.[59]

Diana Butler Bass

Jean is the leader of the finance team of a suburban church named Imagine Church. With an average attendance of 800 people, the church has seen a slight drop in participation in programs and a dramatic drop in giving. Jean and a few of the church's leaders sought my opinion on cutting

---

59 "Reaching for New Metaphors: An Interview with Diana Butler Bass," May 11, 2017, accessed August 22, 2019. http://wildgoosefestival.org/reaching-for-new-metaphors-an-interview-with-diana-butler-bass/.

the budget by 15 percent. Jean was adamant that cutting the budget was the only way to save the church's future.

After inquiring about the giving trend over the past three years, which trended downward, I told her,

"WITH FEW EXCEPTIONS, CUTTING THE BUDGET NEVER LEADS TO GROWTH."

I asked the pastor if he would join our conversation to discuss the church's future. In my interview with the pastor, I wanted to know more about the factors that played a hand in the dramatic drop of the dollars. Here are some of the questions that guided my meeting with the pastor and leaders of Imagine Church:

- **What does your church's ultimate contribution to your community look like?**

- **What guides your most essential priorities along the way?**

- **What singular impact will your church have on your community as the years unfold?**

Acknowledging that my questions were not financial, I asked the group to indulge me further. Listening intently to their responses, I wanted to see if I could *discern* patterns that might give me a clue to the giving downturn. After finding glimpses of some hints, I began to ask the leaders of Imagine Church to *dream* and re-imagine their assumptions about budgets, finances, and stewardship. Learning from my missteps with the Mt. Sinai congregation, this time, I was ready to use inquiring open-ended questions. I started with appreciating what the church did best to help Imagine Church *discern* its past and *dream* of a new financial future. To *dream* of this future, I asked Jean and the other leaders to engage in the following exercise:

A Selfie and Your Church

Take out your cell phones. Individuals who have flip-phones that do not take pictures are exempt from this exercise. Go to your photos. Find a picture of yourself (it can be a "selfie," or an image of you with others in the frame). After everyone has found a picture, then allow the group an opportunity to share the setting and backstory behind the photo. Next, while having the group to focus on the image, especially the selfies, ask the group which person is missing in the picture. For the self-portrait photograph, it will be evident that everyone else is missing since the image is about one person—himself or herself.

After having fun with this exercise, I invited the team to consider if the selfies that they carry on their phones were parallel to the pictures they had of the church. Their photos were all too small. I told them,

YOU NEED A BIGGER PICTURE. YOU NEED A BILLBOARD IMAGE OR MURAL, WHERE PEOPLE WHO ARE NOT CURRENTLY IN THE PICTURE CAN SEE THEMSELVES FITTING INTO YOUR FUTURE PICTURE! ONLY A LARGER PICTURE THAT IS COMPELLING WILL INSPIRE PEOPLE TO GET EXCITED ABOUT YOUR CHURCH'S FUTURE.

Dreaming of and painting a mural-sized image would ensure that Imagine Church's future picture could become a reality. To help them paint the mural, I had to engage in more questions to shift their perspective away from their "selfies."

Imagine Church's current stories were limiting their ability to re-imagine the financial picture for the church. Put another way, Imagine Church needed help in shifting its stories by dreaming of God's preferred future. Oddly enough, the selfie exercise uncovered past accounts of the early days when Imagine was a new church start and prided itself on being a mission-sending church. Sadly, over the years, the waning influence of mission became nothing more than pictures tucked away in back hallways. Like the family portraits where families reminisce about photos in their foyers today, the church's view of missions was limiting. Members could not see past the daunting images of disinterested newer and younger attendees who did not value the church's cherished missionary spirit. Sending people to be life-long missionaries to international countries had become a thing of the past. While a new trend of short-term international missions was emerging, it was difficult for members to raise funds for these trips as they lacked the fanfare of previous experiences.

Given Imagine Church's history of missions, I asked Jean and her team to consider a slight shift in their language about giving. Instead of creating another stewardship campaign, I urged the team to create an "opportunity project."[60] The focus would shift the giving assumptions to more people giving smaller yearly amounts instead of expecting fewer people to give large amounts. Calling it an opportunity project could tie back to the stories of sending missionaries throughout the world, while focusing on the "new world" right outside their doors—their community. As insignificant as it sounded, the shift would also help them to *dream* of God's future picture. Additionally, shifting the language from campaign to an "opportunity project" created a path for Imagine Church members to participate in a unique giving opportunity to fund its mission. An in-depth analysis of stewardship strategies goes beyond the scope of this book. However, I will provide a glimpse behind the assumptions that drive the frequent lack of participation in the campaigns.

STEWARDSHIP ASSUMPTIONS

As we briefly discussed in the introduction, every church has submerged beliefs, the energy that drives behavior. As I look at churches like Imagine Church, recurring patterns emerge that signal submerged feelings which might be at play:

---

[60] The church financial consulting organization, Generis, suggests that to create a generosity lifestyle, the church must shift its language to opportunity projects instead of stewardship campaigns. See Generis, *Accelerating Generosity: How to Create a Culture of Giving in Your Church or Ministry.* eBook. 2017. Accessed September 27, 2019. https://generis.com.

a. The church's struggle with stewardship campaigns;

b. The church's inability to dream of new approaches to fund its mission.

I encouraged Imagine Church to *dream* of what it would look like to re-imagine its submerged beliefs about money and stewardship. More directly, I wanted the leadership to momentarily step off its current path into its submerged assumptions about resources. Here are the questions that I asked which may also be helpful to your team:

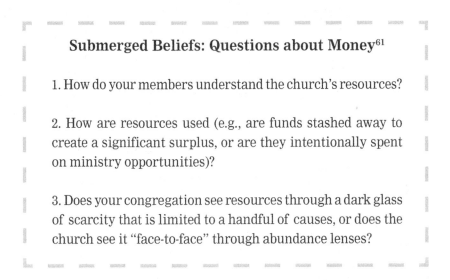

Submerged Beliefs: Questions about Money[61]

1. How do your members understand the church's resources?

2. How are resources used (e.g., are funds stashed away to create a significant surplus, or are they intentionally spent on ministry opportunities)?

3. Does your congregation see resources through a dark glass of scarcity that is limited to a handful of causes, or does the church see it "face-to-face" through abundance lenses?

These questions helped to tease out the team's limiting beliefs surrounding money and resources. To their surprise, the scarcity view that many of the team members shared was not the view of the new, younger families. I encouraged the team to interview some of the younger families, and they were shocked by the responses. To the team's amazement, many younger families were waiting for the church to challenge them about giving and how to manage their resources best. From these insights, I encouraged the team to change the way it talked about giving.

---

[61] Adapted from Edgar Schein's work on the dimensions of a culture where he describes the nature of deeply held assumptions involving the nature of reality and truth, time and space, resources, and human relationships. See Edgar H. Schein, *Organizational Culture and Leadership*, 2nd Edition (San Francisco: Jossey-Bass, Inc., Publishers, 1992), 116.

The team's homework with the pastor was to improve its offering moment. The task was tying giving to the mission by challenging people with compelling personal stories that supported local and global causes. But most importantly, the pastor and church leaders had to be transparent about where the church was spending its money. Sadly, many of the churches that I have visited will miss an essential opportunity to align the offering moment to the mission. Instead of deliberately tying giving to ministry outcomes, many churches assume that people are supposed to give when the offering plate is passed. Depending on the type of church, typically, more attention is given to the choir's anthem than to the people presenting their offerings to God. Here is an example of nonalignment from a pastor's framing of the offering moment at one church I attended:

It's offering time. Will the ushers come forward to receive the morning offering? Please place your tithes and offerings in the offering plate.

In contrast to these churches, other churches capitalize on the offering moment by connecting giving to mission. Here is an example from another pastor's framing:

This past week, your gift helped to provide shelter for forty homeless men. Without your generosity, this would not have been possible. When you give to our church, you are investing in people's lives to make a difference. Thank you for your generosity. In a moment, we are going to allow you to place your gifts into the offering plate. There are three ways for you to participate in the giving moment: placing funds in the offering plate, giving online, and giving by texting. If you were are worshiping with us online, thank you for your gift. Please select the GIVE button on the upper corner of the screen of your mobile device or computer. We give our funds to help to make disciples for Jesus Christ for the transformation of the world. Would the ushers please come forward?

Do you hear the difference between the two? One is generic, and the other takes the time to engage the congregation to connect giving with the church's mission. Which one does your church practice? If your church is like Imagine Church and you are accustomed to the first practice, then a slight modification of telling how gifts given on Sunday aligns with the mission and ministries of the church will take some intentionality. But it can be done. Offering moments happen every Sunday, and so must the alignment of the offering moment to the church's mission. If this does not exist, people cannot connect the dots between why people need to give and how the church spends their gifts.

In some churches, there is a false notion about the offering moment. The thinking goes: *All those big churches have to do is to say, "Will the ushers, please come forward for the morning offering? They do not struggle like us."* Somehow playing a praise song during the offering, so the thinking goes, miraculously makes the offering plates overflow with cash and checks. The faulty conclusion from this type of thinking is that for a church to get more money, it must employ some gimmick. Of course, this is a false notion as I have never seen it happen this way!

Using a slight change in language and addressing the submerged belief questions, as insignificant as it sounds, prompted the team to shift the church's giving patterns. Instead of creating another stewardship campaign, I urged them to call the opportunity project the Imagine Investment Fund. This name would help the Imagine Church's *dream* of unique giving opportunities to fund its mission. Every time a person gives to the church, his or her gift will support the future picture.

Is your church like Imagine Church? More and more, suburban churches suffer from a similar future financial picture, and their program participation may appear to be like the vision of the valley of dry bones: a portrait of decline and profound loss. A quick overview of Ezekiel's story of bare bones will illustrate the necessity of the *dream* process, especially when a church's financial picture becomes blurry.

DREAMING A GOD-DREAM

Ezekiel's dream was to be a priest in the kingdom of Judah. But his hopes and dreams were dashed by King Nebuchadnezzar's invasion, taking him and others captive to Babylon. Separated from the temple in Jerusalem by some 600 miles, Ezekiel's dreams of being a priest had become a nightmare. It was not until Ezekiel was thirty years old that his dream returned, and he began to experience astonishing visions from God:

> In my thirtieth year, in the fourth month on the fifth day, while I was among the exiles by the Kebar River, the heavens were opened, and I saw visions of God.
>
> Ezekiel 1:1 (NIV)

Ezekiel's visions were mostly *God-dreams,* images where God provided gigantic-sized hope-filled murals of a preferred future picture for God's people. Throughout the book that bears his name in the Old Testament, Ezekiel records his *God-dreams* for his people. The image of the dry bones found in Ezekiel 37 is one the most familiar of his *God-dream* pictures of the "what-if" future. This *God-dream* is instructive for churches like Imagine Church that desires a future with a prophecy of hope: the reality of resurrection and restoration for the church's future. The outcome for Ezekiel was a new hope for people who felt overwhelmed by circumstances beyond their control. The Imagine team's challenge was to present a clear picture of how people could experience hope amid their financial turmoil.

THE PICTURE BECOMES CLEAR

Imagine Church's impending financial crisis presented an opportunity for a *God-dream* moment. As I worked with Jean and her team, I encouraged them to begin asking "What if" questions. For example, one of the questions was, "What if your vision for Imagine Church reflected the people living in a community near the church?" Other questions went this way:

- What would happen if you shifted your efforts away from focusing on what you do not have to finding ways to capitalize on your past story of being a mission-sending church?

- What if you framed your financial giving in terms of funding your mission-sending efforts in your local community and short-term missions?

- What if you challenged your people to give an extra $100 per month? Ten percent of the funds will support local and short-term missions, and the remaining 90 percent will go toward the operating cost, debt reduction, and deferred maintenance on the campus?" **After three years of this model, you can switch to 90 percent towards the mission and 10 percent to ongoing maintenance.**

I chose these open-ended *God-dream* questions to help direct the team to envision how the church could align with God's hope for the church and the community.[62] As Jean and her team discovered, a *God-dream* is a compelling vision that is fresh and different, yet somehow familiar. Instead of discarding or diminishing the past, it uses the triumphs of the past to embrace the future.[63] The leaders of Imagine Church emerged from the *dreaming* process with the following statement:

We create a culture of generosity when we:

Imagine a church that is not a place with a program, but a people with a purpose.

Imagine people engaged in serving the community and working for the glory of God.

Imagine a community of ordinary people intentionally living out a mission of generosity and service in our neighborhoods and relational networks of family, friends, business owners, teachers, medical professionals, and students.

Imagine a future when our community identifies our church as a place and people that consistently model the generous life of our Lord and Savior Jesus Christ.

In this chapter, we have walked alongside Imagine Church during its *dreaming* process. In the next chapter, we will focus on the framework that

---

[62] A sample of how your church can utilize a similar process is found in Appendix E: Generosity.

[63] Rev. Cindy Blocksidge, Randy Hardy, and Rev. Dr. Phil Schroeder, *More Than Just One Neighbor,* 2016, 86-87.

supports the *dreaming* process for Imagine Church's program participation problem. In the process, we will be introduced to new concepts along the way to continue to clear debris from the path as we imagine God's preferred future for your church.

GROUP SPIRITUAL PRACTICE

Imagine Church was learning how to *dream* of God's preferred future regarding generosity. In this exercise, your team will begin to *discern* and *dream* about God's preferred future for how you use your financial resources. As you did in the previous spiritual practices, begin by centering yourselves, taking a few deep breaths. With eyes closed, sit in silence for a few moments as you prepare to hear the questions. After a few moments, your guide will begin to read the questions:

1. How does your congregation see its resources? Does it see it through a dark glass of scarcity that is limited to a handful of causes, or does the church see it "face-to-face" through abundance lenses?

2. What would happen if you shifted your efforts away from focusing on what you do not have to finding ways to capitalize on your past story of being a mission-sending church?

3. How might we use these stories of our how our church sees its resources to dream of what God's preferred future is for our church?

After the first question has been asked, sit in silence for ten seconds. One by one each person will invite another member of the group by name to share his or her reflections.

Allow ten seconds of silence after each person has spoken before inviting another to share. If someone chooses not to speak and wishes to pass, this is okay. The person who passes still invites another person, by name, to share. Value each reflection with gratitude, without judgment or agreement.

Remember to honor the ten seconds of silence following each reflection. After each person has had the opportunity to share, you may ask for clarification from one another and begin to dialogue about God's grace-filled possibilities. Repeat this process for the second question. Close your time together with your sentence prayers of praise and thanksgiving. Please allow between twenty to thirty minutes for this process.

7

DREAM

Imagining a New Story

In the last days, God says: "I will pour out my Spirit on all
people. Your sons and daughters will prophesy. Your young
will see visions. Your elders will dream dreams."

Acts 2:17 (CEB)

Many of our churches are slow to adapt and make changes to
engage the times in which we are living—today. We are asking
these churches to examine their current ministry setting and
effectiveness in strengthening existing disciples and reaching
new people.[64]

Candance M. Lewis and Rodney Thomas Smothers

In the previous chapter, we met Jean and the leaders of Imagine
Church who sought to find a solution to their impending financial
crisis. We saw how they began the work of dreaming of a new way to
approach giving.

---

[64] Lewis and Smothers, *Resurgence,* 11.

Along the way, the leaders learned that:

DREAMING IS ABOUT DISCOVERING GOD'S VISION FOR THE CHURCH'S FUTURE AND NOT SETTLING ON THEIR PREFERENCES. TO DREAM IS TO IMAGINE THE GLIMPSES OF GOD'S PREFERRED FUTURE FOR YOUR CHURCH, WHICH IS ACCOMPLISHED BY USING THE SUCCESS STORIES OF THE PAST THAT ARE UNIQUE TO THE CHURCH. DREAM QUESTIONS ARE "WHAT" QUESTIONS THAT HELP YOU TO IMAGINE FUTURE POSSIBILITIES OF THE DISCERNING STORIES.

In this chapter, we will delve further into what it means for your church to *dream*: to seek and receive a *God-dream*.

THE WISH BOOK

In many congregations, *dreaming* feels like looking through the *Sears Wish Book,* the once-popular Christmas gift catalog. The autumn ritual occurred when the *Wish Book* arrived and excited children, eyes filled with wonder, flipped through the catalog looking to circle the desired toy. To save the information for their parents and to refer back to the ideal toy to bide the time until Christmas, kids would dog-ear the page. Many churches still resonate with the *Wish Book* approach to *dreaming* that feels more like nostalgia and not brainstorming, imagining, and asking God to help them think outside the box for a *God-dream*.

Unlike a *Wish Book*, it may be helpful to see the *God-dream* as a leap of faith towards an exciting future that is unfolding. Susan Beaumont uses this perspective through the lens of a popular film, as she writes,

> In the movie *Indiana Jones and the Last Crusade,* Jones comes to the edge of a precipice overlooking a vast abyss, with no obvious way to cross to the other side. His enemies chase him, and he must cross over to save himself and his dying father. A

map in Jones' possession assures him that a bridge exists, but Jones can't see the bridge. He has no choice but to take a single step, a leap of faith, trusting that the bridge is there and will support his weight. He takes one frighteningly bold step forward, and the bridge magically materializes. It was there all along, but Jones couldn't see it from his vantage point.[65]

Perhaps then, our churches can learn the lesson from Indiana Jones, A *God-dream* is not a wish, but trusting that God is present, especially in times when we cannot see him. To receive the *God-dream* is a leap of faith, trust that "the bridge is there and will support us" on our path.

As I worked with Jean and the others, I reminded them that *dreaming* was a leap of faith and *not* copying what the church down the street does. Instead, the goal is to *dream* and communicate the future story of what God is doing in *their* church. Lia McIntosh, Jasmine Rose Smothers, and Rodney Thomas Smothers emphasize the *dream* phase. When talking about imagination and hope in their work, they write,

[To dream is to answer the question]: If you could create anything for your future in the next year, what is it that you'd like to create for your life, your church, or community?" This is a question of imagination, vision, and optimism toward our dreams.[66]

Recapping the team's significant work of getting the bigger picture of the *dream* process, the next step involved creating a broader *Dream Team*.[67] To gain broader acceptance and commitment from the larger church, the team needed to add non-official younger leaders to their ranks. As with my previous encounters with Mt. Sinai's leaders, some of Imagine's members resisted expanding the team. For the first time, the team had to deal with its fears, which ranged from fear of losing status to a crippling fear that

---

[65] Beaumont, *How to Lead*, Location 2379-2380.

[66] Lia McIntosh, Jasmine Rose Smothers, and Rodney Thomas Smothers, *Blank Slate: Write Your Own Rules for a 22nd Century Church Movement* (Nashville: Abingdon Press, 2019), 118.

[67] A dream team is an equivalent of what John Kotter calls a guiding coalition, a group of influential people who can make the dream a reality through leading the change initiative. See John P. Kotter, *Leading Change* (Boston: Harvard Business School Press, 1996), 57.

they would be exposed as imposters who did not know what they were doing. During the impromptu confession, the team also acknowledged that getting buy-in from the larger body would not be easy.

At some point, your church will also reach this impasse that threatens momentum. If your church experiences this hesitancy and resistance, do not push forward. Instead, pause and revisit the *discern* phase to continue inviting stories from the broader membership until they are ready to *dream*. For Imagine Church, it was continuing to visit, asking, "How can we continue in new ways the missionary spirit that once captivated the congregation?" Your church's stories of the past will be unique to its setting and history and will require different questions. Keeping those past success stories before your team will help you frame your questions of how to *dream* a new expression of a previous success story for today.

DREAMING AND OVER-PROGRAMMING

For our purposes, to *dream* means to trust God to give us a future picture of hope. *Dreaming* in the church context is equivalent to a BHAG (bee-hag), a Big Hairy Audacious Goal[68] in the corporate world. According to Jim Collins and Jerry Porras, BHAGs are meant to shift how organizations do business. Collins and Porras describe BHAGs on a corporate level as nearly impossible to achieve without consistently working outside of a comfort zone and displaying organizational commitment, and confidence. For our churches, a BHAG is almost impossible to become a reality unless God steps in and walks the path with us. Imagine Church was the result of Pastor Joshua.

Imagine Church became the BHAG of Pastor Joshua that fueled his passion to birth a church to connect both the de-churched and unchurched people to God. For the previous twelve years of its existence, Pastor Joshua worked tirelessly to recruit a *dream* team of leaders like Jean to help accomplish its mission. By comparison to many of the nearby churches, Imagine Church is still a new church, although it has grown to a large attendance of families with children during its Sunday worship experience.

---

[68] See Jim Collins and Jerry I. Porras, *Built to Last: Successful Habits of Visionary Companies* (New York: Collins Business Essentials; 3rd ed. Edition, 2011).

Since its launch, the church has followed the pattern of creating small groups and programming for various age groups. Every fall, Imagine Church's habit was to start new small groups. But in recent years, like so many of the neighboring established churches, Imagine Church found itself desperately trying to recruit new people to their waning programs. Unbeknownst to its leaders, the church was suffering from an over-programmed and under-discipled malady. Perhaps you have noticed symptoms of this over-programmed malady in your church. Here are signs that you may see:

- **There is something scheduled at the church for every day on the calendar.**
- **The announcement time is just as long as the morning message.**
- **The 80/20 rule, where 20 percent of the people do 80 percent of work is rampant.**
- **There is an exhaustive list of programs without leaders.**
- **The leaders of the church are not aware that a program exists.**

These are just a few examples of the symptoms of being over-programmed that I have encountered. I am sure that you can add to this list. At the heart of over-programming is the misconception that busyness equals growth. To put it more precisely,

ADDING MORE PROGRAMS IS NOT THE CURE-ALL FOR WHAT AILS THE CHURCH.

WHAT ABOUT PROGRAMS?

Up to this point, I have focused all of my attention on a path for churches and not on programs. As we learned in Chapter 3, *Imagine Church,* like most churches, had existing programs with shrinking participation rates. Church consultant Tony Morgan discusses a vital contrast between programs and paths. His thoughts provide insights for addressing shrinking participation rates.

In his book, *The Unstuck Church,* Morgan states that many declining churches have *an overwhelming number of programs* available to attendees and even to the community. But there is not a cohesive path to help people learn which steps to take and when.[69] Churches like Imagine Church fall into the trap of staffing and structuring its team around new ideas and programs. For instance, the church might have a staff member or volunteer oversee the areas of worship, outreach/missions, and discipleship. To continue the growth trajectory of new people, each of these staff persons is encouraged to *dream* of new ideas. On the surface, there is nothing wrong with this structure.

Over time, however, if the church is not intentional about ensuring that all areas align with the mission, this structure creates silos and unwelcomed turf wars for resources. Without the tools of the *discern* and *develop* phases, these churches become stuck in the *dream* phase, where they continually generate ideas without follow through on them.

Volunteers and staff members who serve in this type of church measure success through new ideas generated for ministry, and reports about how many people attended the new ministry program, class, or program, but there is no indicator of spiritual growth. Additionally, this structure also creates an over-dependence on the paid staff to do the heavy-lifting of providing members the opportunity to join a group or activity. Like the Israelites clearing a path through the wilderness to a new *dream* of freedom, people who were once excited about a new program will quickly shrink away from a new idea and revert to their previous reality. People in your church are not any different from the Israelites.

As you continue the *dream* process, you must create a compelling future story that people can understand and embrace. The story of God's preferred future for your church draws a verbal picture of what it looks like to accomplish your mission.

HELPING CHURCHES TO GROW

Several years ago, I participated in a three-day training that focused on the *dreaming* process to help churches grow. The ministry consulting firm

---

[69] See Tony Morgan, *The Unstuck Church,* 134.

Auxano offered the training. The name *Auxano* is the biblical term that means "to cause to grow."[70] In 2004, Auxano's founder, Will Mancini, had to clear a new path of faith that "felt like jumping off a cliff." He confesses,

I had no money in savings, no clients, and no team. But God was calling me to something new, and everything in me wanted to help ministry leaders get the vision right. My holy discontent was driven by exposure to photocopied vision in churches over a 3-year season with a national ministry marketing firm.[71]

Mancini is making a story shift in the church consulting practice by offering a radically different approach to the dream phase of "vision casting." Instead of the traditional "vision casting," he advocates "vision dripping," a metaphor for communicating vision through a soaker hose that slowly drips the water. Said differently, church leaders must always retell the *dream*.

In my work with Imagine Church, I discovered that a future picture does not always come from the audible voice of God or stone tablets, like Moses' experience in the wilderness. Neither Jean nor any of her friends could pinpoint a time when God had audibly answered a prayer request. They could, however, tell stories of how God responded to their petitions through other people.

LOOKING FOR GOD'S DREAM IN YOUR CHURCH IS COMPARABLE TO LISTENING FOR ANSWERS TO PRAYER. GOD'S DREAM FOR YOU WILL COME INTO SHARPER FOCUS WHEN YOU CREATE INTENTIONAL TIME AND SPACE WITH OTHER PEOPLE WHO LOOK FOR HOPE.

Recognizing that *dreaming* about a preferred future does not happen to all people in the same way and at the same time, Pastor Joshua and his

---

[70] Will Mancini, "Clarity Changes Everything: The Meaning of Auxano," accessed September 19, 2019. https://www.willmancini.com/blog/the-meaning-of-auxano.

[71] Ibid.

team retold the *dream* regularly. At every available opportunity, the church connected to the *dream*, including the welcome, offering, announcements, and so on. For your church, as with many other churches, it will take a person hearing your *dream* at least seven times (or more) before he or she hears it once. The repetitive retelling of the *dream* made Jean and the other leaders' "eyes glaze over." Jean and the others were growing weary of hearing the *dream*, but others who were latecomers were hearing the *dream* for the first time. It is just as John Kotter says when leading change: you cannot over-communicate vision or your church's *God-dream*.[72]

THE CLEARER PICTURE

By now, your team may feel a lot like the Israelites in the wilderness. You have gathered information, listened to many stories of the past, and read more reports than you ever thought. You have followed the guidance of the metaphorical day-time cloud pillar and fire pillar during the night. Resembling the people of the exodus in their forty-year ordeal, you may also feel stuck in the middle of the desert and not ready to *dream* anymore. Trapped between the old stories that prompt nostalgia and new stories yet to be told, perhaps you are hesitant to begin *dreaming* about where God is leading.[73] Be comforted in knowing this experience is normal. As you pace yourselves and continue to clear and walk, a new path will emerge.

PART OF THE MOST PAINFUL PORTION OF THE DREAM PROCESS IS THE STRIPPING AWAY OF "EGYPT-SYSTEMS THINKING." THIS TYPE OF THINKING ASSUMES A CAPTIVITY MENTALITY THAT MUST BE RELINQUISHED AS YOU ENTER A SPACE TO SEEK GOD'S POSSIBILITIES AND NOT YOUR INTERESTS.

---

[72] John Kotter, "Think You're Communicating Enough? Think Again," https://www.forbes.com/sites/johnkotter/2011/06/14/think-youre-communicating-enough-think-again/#178b0dfb6275, November 1, 2019.

[73] Gil Rendle notes that the word *exodus* is rooted in the Greek (ex—out of; hodos—way). Exodus offers the image of people taken out of a way of life that was well-known and deeply established leaving them stuck between old and new emerging stories. See Gilbert R. Rendle, *Journey in the Wilderness*, 25.

Remember, *dreaming* requires a metaphorical exodus experience, space, and time commitment to trust God and to walk a path into new and unknown territory. Now that we have completed *dreaming* of God's preferred future for your church, the next step is to develop a process to embody the story. The next chapter will provide insights for your church to develop an action plan along the path.

INDIVIDUAL QUESTIONS FOR REFLECTION

Will Mancini has developed a process called the "vision frame" that helps churches *dream* about a clear vision. I offer the questions[74] from my time with Auxano for your individual reflection.

1. In the space provided, list your *God-dream*, **God's preferred future picture for your church?**

2. What are the dreams and hopes of our church?

---

[74] See Will Mancini and Warren Bird, *God Dreams: 12 Vision Templates.*

3. What is the benefit of attending our church?

4. How do we answer the question "What is in it For Me (WIIFM) for people inside and outside our church?"

8

CROWDSOURCING

Tell Us What to Do

They said to me, "Make us gods who can lead us. As for this man Moses who brought us up out of the land of Egypt, we don't have a clue what has happened to him."

Exodus 32:23 (CEB)

Don't jump in telling answers until you know what the other person really needs to know. Don't assume that the person with the question has asked the right question.[75]

Edgar H. Schein

In the previous chapters, we discussed how your church could begin to *discern* and *dream* about its future. The *dream* about your future will provide a vision of your destination. But how will you get there? What steps will you take? To answer these questions and others similar to them, your church needs to *develop* a plan to help you with practices to make the *dream* a reality.

In this chapter, I aim to help your church answer the "how-to" questions by exploring the final leg along the path: *develop*. But what does it mean to develop? And why is it important to do only after the *discern* and *dream* processes? For our purposes, the *developing* process is the congregation's adoption of the *God-dream* to design new structures more appropriately suited to the church's mission. To develop means to follow James' advice on faith without action:

> **Dear friends, do you think you'll get anywhere in this if you learn all the right words but never do anything? Does merely talking about faith indicate that a person has it? Isn't it obvious that God-talk without God-acts is outrageous nonsense?**
>
> **James 2:14, 17 (MSG)**

Using the *developing* process, we will focus on how an urban church sought to act on its *God-dream* by streamlining its efforts of service to make a lasting impact. I will begin with the church's quest to develop a plan of action by telling the story about two of its members, Denise and Robert, and their desire to serve.

DENISE AND ROBERT

Denise recently married Robert after three years of dating. They got a great deal on a home near what the realtor calls, "an up and coming neighborhood." Located a few blocks away from the city's skyline and high-rise condos, Robert believes the realtor's language is code for purchasing a home in a gentrified neighborhood.

Growing up in a small town before meeting Denise, Robert went to the local bank for transactions and visited the local pharmacy to drop off a prescription. Both the bank and pharmacy were located on the same street a few blocks away from where he lived, and Robert knew the bank president and pharmacist by the first name. Living in a small town provided Robert with a slower pace of life. If there was any traffic, it was on a surface street, and it did not last any more than three minutes (yes, he timed it)!

By contrast, Denise's childhood was the direct opposite of Robert's experience. She spent most of her life in and near large cities. Public transportation was the means of traveling from place to place. And while she knew the owner of the neighborhood corner store, she could also catch a subway train and ride downtown to find larger stores. Denise was familiar with more options than Robert. Though Robert and Denise are from very different backgrounds, they share a common interest: they are passionate about serving to make a local impact.

SERVING FOR HOPE AND IMPACT

Denise and Robert attend Church of Hope. Located on the eastern end of the city, the hundred-year-old church is a fifteen-minute walk from their neighborhood. One reason for attending Church of Hope is its modern worship experience in the sanctuary space of pews and stained-glass windows. They appreciate that people at the church welcome them and are willing to help them encounter God in a way that helps them live out faith in the world.

Church of Hope's attendance size of 200 people conveys the importance of a welcoming community where people can make new friends and nurture friendships. Another reason for attending Church of Hope is for its diverse mix of people who attend on Sundays, including multiracial, multi-income, and multi-generational congregants.

The most compelling reason for Robert's and Denise's attendance at Church of Hope is the church's commitment to service. Like many urban churches, members of Church of Hope want to be a force for good in the community. The church sees its mission as being a place that transforms the lives of all people. Their *God-dream* is to be a church of hope that serves to impact the community. To make their *God-dream* a reality, the church has partnered with twenty-four ministry partners and agencies through the neighborhood.

Denise and Robert realize that the church desperately needs to develop a process to pare down the numbers of service partners. Instead of being like the Cheesecake Factory, which famously boasts over 250 different menu options, they felt like the church needed to become more like a cozy bistro with a limited fixed-price menu.[76] And although the number of partners was cumbersome at times, surprisingly, the majority of members continued to support the partners financially, even if they declined to participate in physical service.

When listening to Denise and Robert share the stories about Church

---

[76] See Matt Miofsky and Jason Byassee, *8 Virtues of Rapidly Growing Churches,* (Nashville: Abingdon Press, 2018), Kindle Edition, Location 405.

of Hope, I discovered how the church took pride in giving $100,000 to their partners to provide hope and make an impact. Despite their generous gifts, I also found that several people gave to their personal preferences. When there was not a partner to fit their liking, the members lobbied the church to add more partners. More often than not, the church granted their petitions. The by-product of their preference selections was that some partners did not receive funding.

THE NEED FOR A PLAN

Denise and Robert were two of several members of the Serve Team, the volunteers who structured the church's service opportunities, to reach out to me. They reported that the needs of the community and partners they sponsored grew to include so many that trying to address all of the demands was sapping them dry. Groping for answers, they were looking for me to tell the church how to manage its service opportunities better. Like the Israelites' demand for Aaron to make a god in Moses' absence (Exodus 32:1-6), Denise and Robert's last-ditched efforts were to meet with me and plead for me to do something to alleviate their anguish. The key to my work with the team was to walk alongside them to develop a plan of action from the *God-dream* of serving for impact in intentional and sustainable ways.

Having learned from my Mt. Sinai and Imagine Church experiences, I resisted the urge to tell them what to do. Instead, I invited them to share their stories. As they began to tell their stories, I intentionally asked the team to reflect on where their notion of service originated. I had a listening ear for the *discerning* process and how their personal stories either clashed with or surfaced the church's submerged beliefs.

By the time that Denise, Robert, and the Serve Team came to me for help, the congregation was burning itself out trying to engage the long list of service partners. I asked them about their service-fatigue and wondered why the church had so many service partners. After some thought, one of the team members remarked, "I guess we believe that bigger is better. And the more you do with the most amount of people, the more impact you make."[77] Without knowing it, the team member had stumbled into an unarticulated

---

[77] "More, more, more" represents a powerful submerged belief from the larger American culture that assumes that "bigger is better," and "winning is everything." See George B. Thompson, Jr. *How to Get Along with Your Pastor: Creating Partnerships for Doing Ministry* (Eugene: Wipf & Stock Publishers, 2006), Chapter 3.

submerged belief! (For a review of submerged beliefs, please refer back to Chapter 1.) Church of Hope's outward-reaching impulse was in contrast to Mt. Sinai's inward-looking orientation, and a balance between inside and outside should be struck.

THE BROAD BRUSH APPROACH

Church of Hope was using a "broad brush stroke" approach to service. Broad brush painting means that the church had an overly general summary of a problem of too many service partners, but they did not have the details or nuance of how to maintain a focused impact through fewer partners.

Though well-intended, the board brush approach was no longer working for the current members. Sadly, service through a broad brush was the only way that the leadership knew to operate. Listening further to the serve team's discussions about their church's history and future story, it became clear that there was a bias for "buffet-style" options present, but the food image does not adequately capture the entire picture. Sure, there was a buffet of options, but what the team was not requesting was more food to solve their problem; instead they wanted help to limit the possibilities.

Redirecting my thoughts to their submerged beliefs of "more, more, and more," another image emerged that describes my experience of the church: crowdsourcing. The way the church had added twenty-four service partners and was open to adding more felt a lot like the crowd-sourcing app waze.[78] Here is why waze popped into my awareness.

CROWDSOURCING

The founders of waze began by asking the question, "What would happen if drivers could pool their experiences in real time on the road to guide one another?" Answering this dream-type question helped waze to develop a venue that offers real-time updates from real-life drivers for

---

[78] waze is a trademarked GPS navigation software owned by Google. To learn more about the waze app, please see https://www.waze.com.

turn-by-turn directions. Using crowdsourced Global Positioning System (GPS) data to map a path around obstacles, waze developed a method of inviting and sharing the contributions of multiple people.

In contrast to the waze app recruitment of more users, Church of Hope blindly followed their story of "more, more, more" without recognizing the toll it was taking on their volunteers. After intently listening to their stories, I asked the Serve Team two dream-type questions: "How might you reimagine your approach to service?" and "What would happen if you had twelve service partners instead of twenty-four?" The team had never thought about this approach.

Looking more intently at their list of partners, I saw a pattern. Four categories of partners focused on economic justice and poverty, homelessness and addiction, and children. The team's work would be to narrow its focus to three partners in the categories. I followed up with a second question to the team: "How might you create a plan to streamline your partners to maximize your time and commitment?" The shift to a three-month focus on one category helps the church focus more time on a group to counter burnout. Additionally, the plan of focusing on one partner per month will help the church live into its *God-dream* of providing hope to impact lives by serving the community.

THE DEVELOP PLAN

The church's plan outlined that one Saturday a month, the church would host a churchwide service day with a partner. The plan was as follows: The Serve Team would work with the church's and partner's calendar to schedule yearly serving opportunities. Continuing the plan, the church would invite one of the twelve service partners to the worship experiences to connect serving opportunities with the church's *God-dream*. The church planned to announce the service on Saturday, and the partner could offer sign-ups after the service. After the activities on Saturday, the church would give an update on the impact made by members serving along with a partner in one of the four categories.

Below is a brief look at the plan the Serve Team developed.

Serve Opportunities:
Making an Impact Through Service

First Quarter Focus: Homeless

January

Name of partner:

Guest Partner Highlight Sunday Date:

Service Saturday Date:

Service Experience Update:

February

Name of partner:

Guest Partner Highlight Sunday Date:

Service Saturday Date:

Service Experience Update:

March

Name of Partner:

Guest Partner Highlight Sunday Date:

Service Saturday Date:

Service Experience Update:

Here is a sample update of what Church of Hope provided to the congregation.

Impact of Hope Highlights

12 Service Partners

150 Volunteers

450 Service Hours

5 adoptions and reunifications

6 GED and High School Graduates

3,000 meals provided and served

100 children received Christmas gifts

5 families moved from homelessness to independence

1 Habitat House built

In the next chapter, we will explore your processes to help your church develop an action plan.

GROUP SPIRITUAL PRACTICE

Like so many long-standing churches, perhaps even yours, Church of Hope had adopted an unspoken policy from their submerged beliefs to serve the needs of its community. Church of Hope developed a plan of action to make its *God-dream* a reality. The plan addressed both member burnout and an unaddressed submerged belief. As your church seeks to develop a plan to make your *God-dream* a reality, you will also need to ask questions about the origin of your submerged beliefs to develop an action plan.

During this group spiritual practice, I invite you to engage your submerged beliefs. Begin by centering yourselves, taking a few deep breaths. With eyes closed, sit in silence for a few moments as you prepare to hear the story. After a few moments, your guide will begin to read the following questions.

1. As you think about how your church serves its community, what are your submerged beliefs that may be driving an unspoken policy? List some of your church's unspoken policies about whom you serve and how often? (For instance, if you provide financial assistance, do you help anyone who walks into your church without any questions? Why?)

2. How can your church's plans of action make your *God-dream* a reality?

After the first question has been asked, sit in silence for ten seconds. One by one, each person will invite another member of the group by name to share his or her reflections. Allow ten seconds of silence after each person has spoken before inviting another to share. If persons choose not to accept the invitation to share at this time, it is okay. The person will invite another person, by name, to share. Value each reflection with gratitude, without judgment or agreement.

Remember to honor the ten seconds of silence following each reflection. After each person has had the opportunity to share, you may ask for clarification from one another and begin to dialogue about God's grace-filled possibilities. Repeat this process for the second question. Close your time together with your sentence prayers of praise and thanksgiving. Please allow up to twenty to thirty minutes for this portion of the exercise.

9

DEVELOP

Creating an Action Plan

To the Jews, I became like a Jew, to win the Jews. To those under the law, I became like one under the law (though I myself am not under the law), so as to win those under the law. I do all this for the sake of the gospel that I may share in its blessings.

I Corinthians 9: 20, 23 (NRSV)

We are now faced with the fact that tomorrow is today. We are confronted with the fierce urgency of now. In this unfolding conundrum of life and history, there 'is' such a thing as being too late. This is no time for apathy or complacency. This is a time for vigorous and positive action.[79]

Dr. Martin Luther King, Jr.

Many churches struggle with understanding the types of problems around them. This misunderstanding has a profound impact. Due to

---

[79] Dr. Martin Luther King, Jr. "Beyond Vietnam, A Time to Break Silence," address given in 1967, accessed November 5, 2019. http://www.informationclearinghouse.info/article2564.htm.

our churches' lack of fully understanding the root issues in our communities, churches often create more significant problems than they solve. Think, for instance, of how people in your church gloss over the connection between discipleship, growing in one's relationship to Christ, and evangelism, sharing the good news to make an impact. In most cases, churches either lump them into one category, or they are exiled to the wastelands of church life. The truth is, the church must include developing a discipleship plan and sharing the good news to impact people's lives.

In the previous chapter, we examined how Church of Hope developed a strategy to turn its *God-dream* of service for impact into reality. In this chapter, we will continue our in-depth exploration of the development phase for your church.

THE DEVELOP PROCESSES USE THE STORIES FROM YOUR CHURCH'S PAST AND YOUR GOD-DREAM TO CREATE A PLAN OF ACTION OF WHAT CAN BE. DEVELOP QUESTIONS ARE "HOW TO" QUESTIONS THAT AID IN DEVELOPING STRATEGIES TO IMPLEMENT THE DREAM.

As you begin to walk the develop portion of the path, I encourage you to review the Community Engagement Questions that we discussed in Chapter 3. Once you have brushed up on the *discern* and *dream* processes using the Community Engagement Questions, you will be ready to *develop* plans to make your *God-dream* a reality.

SERVICE FOR IMPACT

It might be helpful for your church to think of the developing portion as the application phase of the path. As Church of Hope discovered, for a church to move along the discipleship path, something specific and practical has to be done with your *God-dream*. By themselves, dreams do not change our circumstances unless something is done with them.

Oddly enough, some churches will focus all of their energy in the developing phase. You will recognize these churches as the ones who value getting things done so that they can check off the next box. Often these churches fall into the trap of getting stuck in the *development* phase and neglect the *discern* and *dream* phases. When this occurs, people in the pews feel like the Energizer Bunny, the pink mechanical, sunglasses-wearing, flip-flop-wearing toy rabbit that keeps going and going while beating a bass drum for others to follow. Contrary to popular belief, focusing on a lot of activity is not the best model to follow. An alternative model is found with the practices of the early church. The practices of the early church illustrate that when the church neglects to spend time *discerning* through prayer and reflection, asking God for a *God-dream* to implement, the "going and going" energy of the church is drained as its batteries eventually lose their charge.

FROM ANALYSIS TO ACTION

Just as it sounds, the book of Acts records the developing stories of the Apostles' *actions*. You might say that the themes of service for impact are the motivation behind the book. More importantly, the book also hints at the paradigm shift away from the analysis lessons of the disciples, who imitated Jesus' teachings, to the *actions* of the Apostles, who spread Jesus' teachings beyond the walls of Jerusalem.

The Apostles made the shift away from the analysis of the *God-dream* of being witnesses to developing a plan of action and learning how to live out the *God-dream* with the Holy Spirit's power.

IN SIMPLE TERMS, THE APOSTLES MADE THE TRANSITION FROM BEING "ATTACHED FOLLOWERS" TO BEING AMBASSADORS SENT WITH AN ACTION PLAN TO SYSTEMATICALLY RECRUIT AND CONVERT NEW "ATTACHED FOLLOWERS" BEYOND JERUSALEM.

> Do not leave Jerusalem until the Father sends you the gift he promised, as I told you before. 5John baptized with water, but in just a few days you will be baptized with the Holy Spirit. But you will receive power when the Holy Spirit comes upon you. And you will be my witnesses, telling people about me every-where—in Jerusalem, throughout Judea, in Samaria, and to the ends of the earth.
>
> **Acts 1:4-5, 8 (NLT)**

In the language of this book, the Apostles had to make a shift from analysis to action to unearth the roots of overgrown weeds (continued dependence on the Law of Moses) that were blocking "the way" for others to walk the path of connecting people with Jesus. Perhaps a brief exploration of the concept of "The Way" is in order before we discuss the action plan of walking a path.

In Chapter 1, we explored the concept "walk this way" in our discussion about discipleship. It is not by coincidence that "The Way" of Jesus, was also the name of the early Christians during the time of the Apostles. Here, the expression "The Way"—those called to emulate Jesus' behavior—finds its origin in the Hebrew word *halakha* (hal-ah-ka) which means to "walk in his way" and follow in his path.[80] The Way was the process for how the early church responded to God's grace through spiritual practices. These practices helped the followers of "The Way" to attend to God's presence in the world by growing in love.[81] Karen Scheib's voice on spiritual practices is a helpful addition to our discussion of what it means to develop an action plan for the way. She asserts,

> **What we now call spiritual practices are related to what is traditionally the means of grace. The "methods" of grace are channels of how God's grace is made available to us.[82]**

PRACTICES OF THE APOSTLES

According to the Scripture, after Jesus' ascension, the methods of grace were given to the disciples who were left alone in an upper room. During this fifty-day prayer retreat that included discernment, fasting, and praying for a *God-dream*, God answered the Apostles' prayers with the gift of the Holy Spirit:

> **On the day of Pentecost, all the believers were meeting together in one place. Suddenly, there was a sound from heaven like the**

---

[80] Halakha refers to the "way" a Jewish person is directed to behave in every aspect of life, encompassing civil, criminal, and religious law. "Halacha: The Laws of Jewish Life," accessed October 4, 2019. https://www.myjewishlearning.com/article/halakhah-the-laws-of-jewish-life/.

[81] Karen D. Scheib, *Attend to Stories: How to Flourish in Ministry* (Nashville: Wesley's Foundery Books, 2018), 91.

[82] Ibid., 94.

roaring of a mighty windstorm, and it filled the house where they were sitting. Then, what looked like flames or tongues of fire appeared and settled on each of them. And everyone present was filled with the Holy Spirit and began speaking in other languages, as the Holy Spirit gave them this ability.

Acts 2:1-4 (NLT)

The *God-dream* of the promised Holy Spirit provided new energy, empowering the Apostles to become active agents for "The Way." This dynamic, God-infused energy also provided the fuel to develop practices for the establishment of the New Testament churches. After prayerful reflection during the commotion that erupted in the morning, Peter recognized that what appeared to be confusing to the masses was God's action of sharing the *God-dream* promised by Jesus. He stood among the pilgrims and began the *development* phase of providing a plan to embody the *God-dream* (Acts 2:36-39, 41). Peter's analysis and actions jump-started the *development* process of planting new churches beyond the bounds of Jerusalem.

Embodying a *God-dream* to make an impact, the Apostles had received the promised power of the Holy Spirit to tell people about Jesus every-where—in Jerusalem, throughout Judea, in Samaria, and to the ends of the earth (Acts 1:8). In a similar way, the development work of Church of Hope's Serve Team helped them to take a stand of streamlining their service opportunities that provided a way for people to live out the church's *God-dream* of serving to make an impact.

As you look at your church, you may recognize that the development phase is the one that many of your members are most familiar with as the cut-to-the-chase and the bottom-line approach that answers the question, "What are we going to do?" As Church of Hope had to discover, the *developing* process is often the default setting in our churches. The challenge for your church is to not short-circuit the process by ignoring your *God-dream* to put together an action plan.

In the past few chapters, we have walked alongside three churches as they worked to clear a path for discipleship. Along the way, you have been invited to participate in the experiences by *discerning, dreaming,* and *developing* your processes. In the next part of the book, you will work with your team to walk a discipleship path.

INDIVIDUAL QUESTIONS FOR REFLECTION

As you think about developing an action plan to embody your church's *God-dream*, you will need to intentionally create opportunities that help people to act. Part of this process entails helping people move from analysis to action.

Below are questions to assist you in your development plan. If you are unable to list any practices, I invite you to take a closer look at the early church's experiences and spiritual practices of celebrating the Lord's Supper, prayer, and fasting to spur your thoughts on how you might develop more methods for your congregation. For instance, in your church, you may determine that Holy Communion needs more attention. Instead of tacking on the sacrament as an afterthought, you might find ways to be more intentional about giving the ritual equal weight in the worship experience.

1. What are the practices that you observe at your church which help people attend to God's presence and growth in the world? List your practices in the space below.

2. Reflecting on your church's *God-dream* that you discussed at the end of Chapter 5, the story of the early church's beginnings, and the Apostles' actions to develop practices for the churches, how might your church develop a plan of action from your *God-dream*?

3. How does a person who is engaged in your church connect-the-dots between their experience of worship with Bible study and volunteer opportunities?

4. What is your strategy to help a newcomer with the next steps for engagement? There are no right or wrong answers here. Below, list your action plans.

PART TWO
Walking the Path

In this section, we will focus on the reason you purchased the book: to help your church walk the discipleship path. This section will incorporate the *action* portion that is based on the *analysis* framework of Part One. The structure and layout of this part of the book is to be used as a workbook that provides your team with process-centered exercises. It will take a considerable amount of time, and where your church will need to slowly and deliberately work with patience and prayer.

The discipleship path is a journey of transition. Remember that transitions may cause our lives to career off into messy, new, and unexpected directions. You will need to slow down and proceed with caution as you begin to walk the path of this section. There will be twists and turns, false starts and dead ends along the way. When you experience these obstacles, stay the course, knowing that the dust of uncertainty will eventually settle and clear as God is walking ahead of you (Nahum 1:3b).

As I mentioned in Chapter 4, this book does not offer a silver bullet approach with quick and instant results. Instead, your work is a journey that is dependent on the Holy Spirit's movement to challenge, inspire, reveal, and move you.

I have offered five prototypical people to help you explore how your church can engage them through Worship, Serve, Grow, Give, and Impact opportunities. When following the path of discipleship outlined here, your goal is to strive to help your church fulfill their membership vows to be faithful to the church by their Prayers, Presence, Gifts, Service, and

Witness.[83] The outcome of Worship is Presence, Serve is Service, Grow is Prayers, Give is Gifts, and Impact is Witness. I suggest using the same team as before, which includes the pastor and the same twelve people you used in the Part One to engage in this process. Even if your team is not yet ready to engage in all of the practices, you may return back to the analysis section of Part One until you are ready to move forward.

As you work through your questions, you may begin to get antsy and struggle with the fear of not doing this exercise correctly. These are normal feelings that every church will encounter in the process. Remember that the process involves listening for stories and finding patterns. This is not an exercise for focusing on "getting things right." The focus is for you to pay attention to the stories in front of you and work alongside people like William, Susan, Gary, Gwen, and Isaac to help them grow in the practices of discipleship. You can expect that the process with each person will take up to more than two or three sessions, so buckle your seat belts for a long journey. And while it might feel like a long time, if discipleship is to be a life-long journey, then helping people to successfully make a life- changing transition will be well worth it.

Along the way, your team may also be tempted to skip over the methods of *discerning* (praying) and *dreaming* (brainstorming) and go immediately to *developing* (planning). In such cases, please remind your team that your task is to resist the temptation. Staying the course and working through every phase will help you to create a discipleship path unique to your church's context. It will be hard work for your team, but with God's help, you can complete it.

Finally, before your team begins the process, it may be helpful to remind you of the outcome of the discipleship path: making disciples who give attention to God's **Presence** by participating in corporate worship experiences, who **Serve** inside and outside the church wall, and who grow through **Prayer** by investing their time, talents, and financial **Gifts** to demonstrate a faithful **Witness** to others. For a graphical representation of the discipleship path, I invite you to look at the Appendix under Discipleship Path. Let's get started walking the path.

---

[83] These are the membership vows for every member who belongs to a United Methodist Church. For more information, please see "Our United Methodist Vows," accessed November 20, 2019. http://www.umc.org/topics/our-united-methodist-vows/.

10

WORSHIP

Honoring God Daily

Therefore, I urge you, brothers and sisters, in view of God's mercy, to offer your bodies as a living sacrifice, holy and pleasing to God—this is your true and proper worship.

Romans 12:1 (NIV)

Worship is about giving honor and glory to God. At a corporate level, worship is the gathering of the community of faith to praise God, learn the ways of God, and be challenged to take the next steps in our commitment as disciples. At a personal level, worship is about living life in a way that honors God in all that we are and do.[84]

Phil Maynard

William is 55 years old. He is from another denomination but had a bad experience. He has attended your worship experiences

---

[84] Phil Maynard, *Shift 2.0: Helping Congregations Back into the Game of Effective Ministry* (Knoxville: Market Square Publishing Company, LLC., 2018), 71.

sporadically on the so-called big Sundays of Christmas, Mother's Day, and Easter. Your team wants people like William to have a meaningful worship (prayer, praise, giving teaching, and service) experience at your church. Your goal for William is to help him honor and worship God. You also want William so engaged that he begins to invite others to worship. To arrive at this goal, you will have to create steps that help to increase William's attendance patterns from attending only on "the big three Sundays" to attending regularly. Of course, you will also have to define how many Sundays your church considers "regular attendance." Will it be three out of four Sundays, twice a month, or once per month? Once per month is what several churches now consider "regular attendance."[85]

THE WORSHIP EXERCISES

The exercises below will allow your team to *discern, dream,* and *develop* processes to help people like William walk the discipleship path in the area of Worship. The exercises are meant to keep the connection between the *discern* and *dream* processes together.

As I said earlier in the book, this is a not a quick-fix process that provides a "how to tell you what to do" plan. Instead, this chapter and the remaining chapters in Part Two place emphasis on the "how to" parts of the lengthy *discerning* and *dreaming* process. It might be helpful for your team to think of this process as brainstorming sessions to *discern* creative ways to help William.

At every step along the way, I will suggest sample questions for you to ask that will help William imitate the practices on the path. Starting with sporadic worship, you will create longterm methods to help William move to the practice of regular worship. From attending worship regularly, the next exercise is for William to practice daily moments of worship that include loving others. Finally, your task is to help William move from weekly moments of worship to the goal of honoring and worshiping God every day and inviting others to a corporate worship experience.

---

[85] See "Attendance at Religious Services," accessed October 24, 2019. https://www.pewforum.org/religious-landscape-study/attendance-at-religious-services/.

PRACTICE #1: ATTENDING WORSHIP SPORADICALLY

To help William move from attending your church sporadically, you are encouraged to find ways to help him to imitate **Practice #1: Attending worship regularly.**

DISCERN

Your team will start the process by *discerning* the underlying reason for why William attends worship sporadically and why he might want to attend your church regularly. Remember that the *discern* process is a prayerful and deliberate process which involves asking, seeking, and knocking to hear the stories that make your church and the people who attend it tick (Matthew 7:7).

To begin the process, you will want to listen to William's story to begin to understand what makes him tick. It might also be helpful for you think of answering the WIIFM? question for William. In other words, what will William possibly see as benefits to himself to begin attending worship more regularly? Note that this is a starting question and not the only question that your team should consider. For instance, you might consider asking why William only attends three services a year? Is this a holdover from his family of origin? What caused the bad experience in the other denomination, and why did it drive him away from the church?

In the space below list the reasons for **why William might change his behavior and become a regular attendee during the church's worship experience.** After a few sessions of your team connecting with William, begin to build William's trust of the group through group exercises of inviting others to share their life stories during the first 10 minutes of your team gathering sessions. In addition to your group time together, to continue the trust-building process, you might also consider asking the group to meet for lunch, coffee, or dinner, or to visit a park or an athletic event outside the official group time.

As you begin to think about why William might change his behavior, it may be helpful for you to review the Community Engagement Questions in Chapter 3, thinking of ways to use them with William and other members of the group to hear their hopes, dreams, and desires.

Once you discover these items, write them down and spend some time *discerning* whether or not your current worship experience does or does not address these needs.

D R E A M

After *discerning* the stories behind why William wants to change, your team will work to *dream* of meaningful worship experiences that will help him go beyond worship on Sundays. Before engaging in this part of the process, it might be helpful to remind the team that the *dream* phase is a creative brainstorming phase that requires a leap of faith to imagine glimpses of God's good and pleasing, preferred future picture (Acts 2:7).

Here is the *dream* phase question that you will consider. As you did previously, gather your team to spend some time dreaming about the desired outcome, considering this question: **What would happen if we engaged William before, during, and after worship to make his experience of worship more meaningful?** As you ask this question, you might anticipate a wide list of varying responses. At this point, jot them all down and go back to the *discern* process to determine if there is a pattern to the group responses. In the spaces below, list all the groupings of new approaches to worship that your church can *dream* of that will engage William in meaningful ways. Consider several options for your *dreaming* phase. For instance, you may need to imagine new ways to connect with new guests by rethinking your website. You may also need to re-imagine your hospitality practices of welcoming and following up with guests.

DEVELOP

The final step toward the everyday practice of attending worship regularly is for your church to *develop* **an intentional plan to make William's experience more meaningful to him in his daily life.** This step will take more time for creative and collaborative thinking and planning. It will require your team to spend considerable time to "count the cost" of the resources that it will take to accomplish the plan (Luke 14:28). I encourage your team to spend time evaluating all of the opportunities to pursue before making any concrete plans. After you list all possibilities, begin to sort the ideas to determine if patterns emerge for grouping together. From the grouping, list two or three plans, including a timeline for completion and a person to be responsible for implementing and reviewing the action plan.

In the space below, write out your action plan.

After your church has completed the long process of creating a plan that encourages William (and other people like him) to participate in regular worship, the next practice in the process is to help William create daily moments of worship that move him to love others and invite them to worship. Just as when you worked through the steps to create the first practice, it will take some time to create steps to the second practice. You will want to monitor the pace of your process.

PRACTICE #2: DAILY WORSHIP AND LOVING OTHERS

William attends your worship experiences regularly. How will you help him imitate **Practice #2: Creating daily moments of worship, loving others, and inviting people to worship.**

DISCERN

The first step towards this practice is to *discern*: **What are the potential reasons why William would want to move beyond regular worship to daily worship outside of the church? Why would he want to love others?** Follow the same process as you did before of prayerfully and deliberately asking, seeking knocking, and listening to William's

116

stories to *discern* a pattern. In the spaces below, list all the potential reasons why William would feel compelled to move beyond attending regular corporate worship to practice daily worship?

DREAM

Your next step with William is to **dream about what would happen if your church created ways for William to have meaningful worship experiences beyond Sundays?** As in every dream phase, you will need to brainstorm about the various options without settling on the first idea that comes to mind. In your group, take time to ponder the possibilities and record your thoughts. In the spaces below, list all the new possibilities that you can create to help William have meaningful worship experiences beyond Sunday mornings.

DEVELOP

After you have discovered ways for William to have meaningful worship experiences beyond Sunday mornings, your team will need to develop tangible ways for William to live into your *God-dream* by **helping him to worship beyond Sundays, to invite others to begin worshiping daily, and to love others.** Remember that this is not a quick fix, but an engaging process of asking and not telling. List the processes that you will need to follow to help William reach your goal.

Following the same pattern of developing an action as you did in the first practice with William, your team is invited to create two or three action plans to help William worship beyond Sunday and invite others to worship. You might consider creating a process that helps William to make worship (prayer, praise, and giving) a lifestyle.

Here are some of the actions you might consider:

- **Start the day with God. Before getting out of bed, spend five minutes thinking about the blessing of knowing that God will be present in every part of your day.**

- **Throughout your day, watch for and write down answers to prayer. Notice the variety in creation. Pay attention to the ways God is working around you. Celebrate who God is and all God does.**

- **Set aside fifteen minutes during the day where you will absolutely refuse to be negative. Surrender any grumbling and complaining to God.**

This is not an exhaustive list, and I am sure that once your team begins to brainstorm, you will think of more to add to the list. Write new ideas below.

WORSHIP OUTCOME: PRESENCE—HONORING AND WORSHIPING GOD

The next task is for your team is to *discern, dream,* and *develop* practices to help William reach the outcome of discipleship in the area of worship: **honoring and worshiping God every day and inviting others to worship experiences.**

DISCERN

To achieve this outcome your team will need to *discern* a process **to move beyond daily worship and loving others to inviting others to worship.** List any ideas that you and your team share.

DREAM

Next, your team will need to *dream* of new possibilities that might aid your church in helping William to love others and invite them to worship. The question that you will need to explore is, **"What would happen if our church had a process to help William love others and invite them to worship?"** List below the results of your brainstorming session of creative ways to help William.

DEVELOP

Finally, your team will need to engage in last step of the *develop* process to address the following question: **"How can we create processes to help William worship beyond Sundays and invite others to meaningful worship?** At this point, your team will need to think about a tangible structure that will help William and others along the path of discipleship to reach your worship outcome. You will want to consider how your team will coach William on how to invite people to church.

You might begin by using a few questions from the Community Engagement Questionnaire from Chapter 4 to help you engage new people outside your church's wall. You will want to train William on how to ask non-threatening, open-ended questions to new people who attend church events which are based on the needs from your own findings from the questionnaire. You will also want to teach William how to remain curious and open to listening to others and honoring their stories of hope. After sharing stories, you will want William to invite the person to the next activity to further develop a genuine interest in getting to know the person. During the next activity, William will need to connect the new person to people in his sphere of influence who share similar interests and dreams and then invite them to attend worship on Sunday. Of course, this is one of many ways of using the engagement process with which your team will be familiar to invite others to worship. As your team considers its unique culture and *God-dream*, you will discover more ways to accomplish the goal. List your process below.

11

SERVE

Leading by Serving

You know that those who rule the Gentiles show off their authority over them and their high-ranking officials order them around. But that's not the way it will be with you. Whoever wants to be great among you will be your servant. Whoever wants to be first among you will be your slave—Just as the Son of Man didn't come to be served but rather to serve and to give his life to liberate many people."

Matthew 20:25-28 (NRSV)

Christian service leads to a transformation of all involved. The barriers between the haves and have nots, between the ones offering service and the ones receiving service, have less and less meaning and relevance.[86]

J. Patrick Vaughn

Susan is a 40-year-old married mom with two kids. She wants to be a "good" person and wonders how she can make a difference in the world.

---

[86] J. Patrick Vaughn, *Meeting Jesus at Starbucks: Good News From Those Done with Church* (Chapin: Pinnacle Leadership Press, 2018), 81-82.

Your church wants people like Susan and her friends to find meaning in their lives through serving others. Like all of the exercises in this section, there are no quick fixes, and it will take time (up to two years) for your team to create and refine the process. Your goal for Susan and others like her is for her to restructure her life and resources to lead by serving others. You will also want Susan so engaged in serving that she begins to invite others to serve inside and outside your church walls. To arrive at this goal, you will need to create inspiring opportunities that equip Susan to volunteer inside the church and in the surrounding community.

THE SERVE EXERCISES

The exercises below will allow your team to use the 3D-Journey to *discern, dream,* and *develop* a process to help Susan in the area of service. As the name "journey" suggests, these exercises will not provide a quick-fix solution for Susan. Instead, your team will continue to engage in several brainstorming sessions to *discern* creative ways to help Susan. At every step along the way, I will suggest sample questions for you to ask that will help Susan imitate the practices on the path.

Just as you did with William in the last chapter, the exercises below will guide your church in the process of *discerning, dreaming,* and *developing* practices that will help people like Susan walk the discipleship path in the area of service. It is helpful to remember that your work is to *discern, dream* and *develop* practical steps that your church can provide to help Susan serve. As with William and others, this will be an ongoing process to keep Susan involved and growing toward the goal of making Service a lifestyle for her. Beginning with Susan's desire to make a difference, your team will gather once again to begin the process of creating steps to help Susan move toward the practice of serving inside and outside the church walls.

Your team will want to intentionally prepare a series of movements and practices of engagement for Susan. Once you have created the series of movements for service engagement, the next series of movements is to help Susan to begin using her gifts, talents, and passions to make a difference daily. Lastly, your objective is to help Susan move to the outcome of restructuring her life to follow Jesus, to lead by serving others, and to invite others to serve.

PRACTICE #1: SERVING INSIDE THE CHURCH AND THE COMMUNITY

To begin the process of getting Susan to serve others, your team will want to help her imitate **Practice #1: Serving inside and outside the church walls.**

DISCERN

At each step of the way of helping Susan with the practice, pay attention to her stories and *discern* any patterns that might give your insight into Susan's desire to serve. The question for your team to consider is, **"Why should Susan change her behavior?"**

As you sit together with your team, begin talking through the questions, and list your findings below.

DREAM

Over time, your team will continue to *discern* why Susan wants to change. After you have plumbed the depths of the discernment process, your team will begin to brainstorm and *dream* of all the serving opportunities inside and outside your church that will engage Susan's interest and passion. (As you imagine the possibilities, at some point much later in the *develop* phase, your team will want to create an inventory of gifts, interests, and passions that match the serving opportunities in your church).

One question to help guide you could be, **"What would happen if we made all service and volunteer experiences more meaningful to Susan and anyone else in our church?"** Consider several options to *dream* about. List below all of the possibilities in your *God-dream* for new volunteer opportunities.

DEVELOP

From the list of your *dream* opportunities, gather together as a team, and create a plan that makes the *dream* of serving a reality. Use this question to guide your steps: "How do we make Susan's service experience more meaningful? "

Once your team diligently works through the process of walking along-side Susan as she begins to join others in volunteering, you will want to create a reflection process that connects the dots to provide her with clarity and the purpose of serving. From her experience as a volunteer for action and from the reflection process, Susan will begin to see a clear path to walk and will practice serving inside and outside the church walls. The next practice for Susan will be to use her gifts and talents to make a difference on a daily basis.

PRACTICE #2: USING GIFTS, TALENTS, AND PASSIONS

DISCERN

Now that Susan serves the church through volunteering and engaging in service projects in the community, your team will want to brainstorm *(discern, dream,* and *develop)* ways to help Susan imitate **Practice#2: Using her gifts, talents, and passion to make a difference on a daily basis**. In the spaces listed below, your team needs to *discern* **a reason why Susan might potentially want to move beyond serving in the church on Sundays to make a daily difference.**

D R E A M

Your team will go through the process of addressing the question for *dream:* **"What would happen if we made Susan's experience of making a difference daily more meaningful?"** List the possibilities below.

DEVELOP

Using the ideas from your *dreaming* session, your team will begin to address the *develop* question: **"How do we make Susan's difference making more meaningful?"** List your responses below.

SERVE OUTCOME: SERVICE—LEADING BY SERVING AND INVITING OTHERS

DISCERN

To assist Susan's progress toward the outcome of restructuring her life and resources to lead by serving and inviting others to serve, your team will need to *discern, dream,* and *develop* a process by first answering this question: **Why would Susan potentially restructure her life and resources to lead by serving and inviting others?** Below, list all of reasons that Susan might consider this shift in behavior.

129

D R E A M

To help Susan progress toward the goal, your team will *dream* of the possibilities that will help her to lead by serving others. ***Dream:*** **What would happen if we made Susan's experiences of leading by serving others more meaningful?** As you brainstorm, remember that your task is not to place value on your ideas. At this point, consider several options for the *dreaming* process. Resist the urge to dismiss any idea that comes from the *dreaming* process. List your responses below.

DEVELOP

The next step in this process invites your team to engage in *developing* a plan that encourages Susan to restructure her life and resources to serve others. Just as in the other *develop* phases, your team should expect to spend a considerable amount of time putting together a plan. The question you will be addressing is this: **How will you help Susan to structure her experiences of leading-by-serving so that they are more meaningful to her?**

Below, record your team's thoughts.

Congratulations! By working alongside Susan on her leading-by-service journey, you are well on your way of having a path for Susan and others to serve inside and outside the church walls. Along the way, I hope that your team has developed the discipline of incorporating the action and reflection processes into each of your service and volunteer activities. Without this discipline, it will be difficult for Susan, and others like her, to connect dots between participating in service projects and the bigger picture of why it is important to follow Jesus' command to lead by serving others (Matthew 20:25-30). In the next chapter, we will work to help Gary grow in the practices of faith on the discipleship path.

12

GROW

Practices of Faith

The fundamental fact of existence is that this trust in God, this faith, is the firm foundation under everything that makes life worth living. It's our handle on what we can't see. The act of faith is what distinguished our ancestors, set them above the crowd.

Hebrews 11:1-2 (MSG)

Unless a congregation reconnects faith with context in a fresh and powerful way, no strategy, structure, or program will make much difference in its long-term viability.[87]

Alice Mann

Gary is a 65-year-old who has more time on his hands than ever. He occasionally prays for family members who are experiencing health concerns and life crises. Gary has never read the Bible, but he is intrigued by God's story and prayer. He is distant in worship. He does not bow his

---

[87] Alice Mann, *Can Our Church Live? Redeveloping Congregations in Decline,* (Lanham: Rowman and Littlefield Publishers, 2014, Kindle Edition), 62.

head during prayer time and has a blank stare on his face when everyone else closes their eyes. Your team is curious about Gary's behavior, but you do not know how to engage him. In addition to this, your team does not want to offend him or others who follow a similar practice. Your church's goal is to *discern, dream,* and *develop* practices to help Gary engage in the spiritual practices that encourages him to grow closer to God so that he can encourage others in the same way.

THE GROW EXERCISES

Just as you did in Chapters 10 and 11, your team will once again engage in the exercise of asking and listening to stories. In this case, you will be listening to Gary so that you can journey alongside him as he grows in the spiritual practices of faith. Along the way, you will want to follow the same process for Gary as you did for William and Susan in walking the 3-D Journey of *discerning* (praying), *dreaming* (brainstorming), and *developing* (planning).

PRACTICE #1: BECOMING CLOSER TO GOD

DISCERN

To address this concern, your team will need to help Gary imitate **Practice #1: Becoming closer to God through prayer and Bible study.** Reaching this goal requires that your team provide a process to allow Gary to grow closer to God. You will begin by engaging the *Discerning* process of listening to Gary's story. Consider this question: **Why does Gary feel far from God, and why would he potentially change the behavior that makes him feel like this?**

As you listen to Gary's story, remember that your goal is to discover the ebb and flow of his story to help you understand why he prays only occasionally and what would prompt a change from this behavior. List your reasons why he might feel far from God and why he would be willing change.

Consider what it may mean to him to "feel far from God."

D R E A M

The next phase of the journey for your team is to *dream* of new ways that make prayer meaningful for Gary. In your work together, consider this guiding question: **What would happen if we made experiences of prayer and Bible study at our church more meaningful for Gary?** As you begin the *dreaming* process, here are a few questions to guide you along the way:

- **What are some various methods of prayer that your church might consider that may be more engaging for Gary?**

- **Would a guided responsive prayer be helpful to Gary?**

- **Does your church have a beginner's level Bible study that is non-threatening for people who are not familiar with reading the Bible?**

As you might imagine, you will discover several options to make your *God-dream* for Gary become a reality. List your dreams below.

D E V E L O P

Now that you have ideas about the reasons that Gary would potentially change and a *dream* (picture) for him to pursue, this phase of the journey will require your team to spend time considering the *develop* question: How do we encourage Gary in his faith by making the spiritual disciplines of prayer and Bible study experiences more meaningful to him? Similar to the process that you followed with William and Susan, your team will need to consider a plan of action to guide Gary.

One practice that you might consider in your planning is to create a PARB, which stands for Plan, Action steps (list no more than five), Review (feedback on how the process is working and what, if anything, needs to be added or omitted), and Benefit (the outcome of the plan). The idea is for you to brainstorm a plan that consist of two or three action steps. After working through the action steps, you will want to review the progress to determine if the plan was beneficial to Gary. Once you have completed your PARB for Gary, list all of the steps that you need to help Gary embrace a rewarding prayer life.

Great work! As Gary begins to practice the actions that you provided through the PARB process, he will begin to immerse himself in Bible study and praying for others on a more consistent basis. Though he may still forget to pray at times, or his mind may wander when he prays, he is beginning to see the benefits of a prayer life. Additionally, Gary is finding that, through prayer, he does not feel as far away from God as he once did.

PRACTICE #2: DAILY GROWING CLOSER TO GOD

Your next step is to create methods to help Gary imitate **Practice #2: Growing closer to God.** Just as you did before, your team will need to begin with listening to Gary's stories.

DISCERN

This time your task will be to listen for new experiences of prayer and ponder what is next for Gary that will help him grow closer to God. One logical place to begin is with Bible study so that he begins to learn about God. Consider this guiding question during your discernment: Why would Gary want to engage in Bible study and prayer groups? List your ideas in the space below.

DREAM

Spend time with praying and dreaming about this question: **What would happen if you made Bible study and group prayer more meaningful for Gary?** As you work together, consider your existing Bible study experiences and whether or not Gary will be a good fit in your classes. Will he feel at home in your classes? In doing this, now may also be a good time to *dream* about new Bible study opportunities for your church. For prayer groups, consider if your prayer groups would be easy for a newcomer like Gary to participate.

List your *dreams* below:

Gary is beginning to attend a Bible study class and is finding it exciting and rewarding. He is meeting new friends who want to know more about his story and how they can walk alongside him and pray for him. Before his involvement in this class, Gary could not have imagined that people would be genuinely interested in him and his story.

DEVELOP

Your next task is to *develop* a plan that helps Gary form deeper relationships during Bible study and group prayer. Consider this guiding question: **How can we make Bible study and group prayer experiences more meaningful for Gary by fostering relationships that encourage spiritual growth?** Based on your current study and prayer opportunities, and what you have learned from Gary, how can Bible study be more engaging for him and others? List the ways to *develop* a process to promote meaningful Bible study experiences.

GROW OUTCOME: PRAYER—INVITING OTHERS TO LEARN SPIRITUAL PRACTICES

DISCERN

From the results of your work with Gary, he is now growing closer to God by engaging in Bible study and prayer practices on a daily basis. Your next task is to help Gary move toward the outcome of the discipleship path in the area of growth: To invite others to learn spiritual practices in which they can grow closer to God. Consider this question: **Why would Gary want to help others learn spiritual practices so that they can grow closer to God?** Below, list the reasons that Gary might see the benefits of spiritual practices in his life.

D R E A M

Next, using the guiding question, begin to *dream* about **what would happen if we made experiences of inviting others to learn about spiritual practices more meaningful for Gary?** Here is where your team can use its imagination to *dream* outside of the box. What new spiritual practices can you offer to help Gary and others continue to grow in their daily spiritual practices? Consider these as a few suggestions: a Labyrinth, fasting, or praying the scripture through the practice of Lectio Divina (guided prayer). The possibilities are endless. List your *dreams* below.

DEVELOP

Finally, your team gets the chance to put your *dreams* for Gary into practice. Consider this guiding question: **How do we make experiences of deeper spiritual practices more meaningful for Gary and others?** List your action plans below.

The result of your team's work together is helping Gary to move along the discipleship path of **becoming closer** to God. He wants other people to experience the closeness that he enjoys. Gary's relationship with God moves him to invite others inside and outside the church to become involved in spiritual practices. Gary is especially drawn to people who feel far from God, just as he once felt.

Your goal in this part of the process is to provide ways for Gary to become ready to champion spiritual practices that encourage others who feel far away from God to grow in their faith through prayer, Bible study, fasting, and so on. By doing so, Gary begins to practice his faith in tangible ways that others can imitate and experience. As he grows in daily practice, his spiritual muscles will continue to get stronger because of his disciplined exercise regime which has positive effects on how he lives, works, and plays.

13

GIVE

Investing Resources

Give, and it will be given to you. A good portion—packed down, firmly shaken, and overflowing—will fall into your lap. The portion you give will determine the portion you receive in return."

Luke 6:38 (CEB)

Most churches have a God-sized [dream] but are left paralyzed wondering how to fund the [dream].[88]

Generis

G wen is a single 32-year-old with college loans. She is a new attendee at your church but feels awful that she cannot put any more than three dollars in the offering. She does her best to make ends meet, but the cost of living and repayment of college loans is more than her entry-level job pays. In lay terms, her "out-go" (expenses) is more than her "income" (revenue), and that causes her "upkeep" (money management) to become her "downfall" (not enough money). She has a lot of debt and receives

---

[88] "Fund the Vision: Short-term Tactics vs Longer-term Planning," accessed October 15, 2019. https://generis.com/fund-the-vision.

funds of support from her parents. She knows that she needs to manage her finances, but she is not sure how. Ever since she can remember, Gwen's parents have provided a financial safety net to keep her from falling into the pit of bank overdrafts. To help her offset her mounting student loan debt, Gwen's parents allowed her to stay at home during college instead of living on campus. Additionally, Gwen was able to use a family car that was passed down to her when her parents purchased a new one. Gwen's parents are encouraging her to learn how to monitor what she spends, hoping that someday that she will be independent and off of her parents' "pay roll."

THE GIVE EXERCISES

Because you will be helping Gwen to make a transition from debt to generosity, your team will spend a considerable amount of time developing this process. As in the other scenarios, you can expect the entire process to take up to nine months or more. As you prepare for this journey with Gwen, you will need to consider how you will walk alongside her on the path of *discerning, dreaming,* and *developing* practices to help her learn to give financially on a regular basis and to give sacrificially with her time and talent so that she will begin to invite others to give.

As in the previous areas of the discipleship path, your team will start by paying attention to Gwen's story. A good place to start is to ask inquiring questions about creating a space for Gwen to share her story in a non-threatening way in a safe environment. Your team might try introducing a grace margin as a spiritual practice (see Chapter 2 for a review of the practice) as a way to hear and honor Gwen's story of debt without passing judgment.

PRACTICE #1: OCCASIONAL GIVING

Gwen is eager to become a faithful member who gives ten percent of her income to the church. Given her current financial picture, however, she sees that this is an impossible task. Your team will walk through the process of helping Gwen move from financial debt to imitating **Practice #1: Giving occasionally in worship and to special causes.**

DISCERN

To help Gwen begin this practice, your team will need a process to help her to manage her finances and debt. You will need to spend some time *discerning* the root causes of Gwen's debt. Does Gwen live with a submerged belief of scarcity, believing that she will never have enough money? How was money talked about in her parents' home? Engaging these and other questions will help you to *discern* **why Gwen has debt and what could be done to change the behavior at the root cause of her debt?**

List your thoughts in the space below.

DREAM

The next step is to *dream* (brainstorm) about new possibilities that can help Gwen with money management. As you begin the process, you will need to recall the stories of Gwen's relationship with money, and perhaps *discern* how her operative narrative might be at play. (See Chapter 2 to review the power and influence of the operative narrative.) Begin to wonder about the following questions: **What would happen if you made Gwen's experiences of giving more meaningful by offering biblical approaches to**

resolve debt? It might be helpful to review Chapters 5 and 6 with Imagine Church to refresh your memory about the *discernment* process.

Using the group spiritual practice of grace margin, invite your team to gather together in a circle and take a few deep breaths. With eyes closed, sit in silence for a few moments. Your guide will begin to read the following question:

What can we do to paint a picture big enough that Gwen can see herself participating in giving, even though she struggles with money?

After the question has been asked, sit in silence for ten seconds. One by one each person will invite another member of the group by name to share his or her reflections. Allow ten seconds of silence after each person has spoken before inviting another to share. If someone chooses not to speak, and chooses to pass, this is okay. The person who passes still invites another person to share. Value each reflection with gratitude, without judgment or agreement.

Remember to honor the ten seconds of silence following each reflection. After each person has had the opportunity to share, you may ask for clarification from one another and begin to dialogue about God's grace-filled possibilities. Repeat this process for the second question. Close your time together with sentence prayers of praise and thanksgiving, and list your *dreams* below.

D E V E L O P

Finally, you will need to *develop* a plan that encourages Gwen to give. Will your church offer a debt reduction class based on biblical principles? How will you organize your offering moment so Gwen does not feel that your church is always asking for more money? These examples are the tip of the iceberg. Consider this question to guide you through the process: **How can we make Gwen's experiences of resolving debt so meaningful that she is empowered and encouraged to give?** A word of caution is due here. In empowering and encouraging Gwen to give, you do not want to run the risk of coming across as manipulative. Nor do you want to infer a prosperity gospel mentality of giving to get something in return. Your aim should be to strike a balance between encouraging Gwen to resolve debt so she can live into her own *God-dream* of being a generous giver.

It might be helpful for you to review Imagine Church's opportunity project in Chapter 6 to help spur your thoughts so that you can put together a manageable plan. Develop a plan and a way to evaluate the results to help Gwen feel encouraged the next time she attends your church. Ready? Set? Go. List your development plans below.

PRACTICE # 2: GIVING TEN PERCENT

Now that you have provided ways for Gwen to give occasionally and to special causes, the next step for your team is help her imitate **Practice#2: Regularly giving ten percent of resources, time, and talents.**

DISCERN

This *discern* question will help guide you through this process: **Why would Gwen move beyond occasional giving or giving to special causes?** Are there local causes beyond your awareness? What causes excite Gwen and encourage her to give? List your thoughts below.

Your church will need to continue to discover ways to help Gwen manage her money and give to special causes for which she is passionate. Does your church offer financial management courses to help others learn about giving from a biblical perspective? Does your church offer partnerships like those of Imagine Church (Chapter 5) for you to highlight as ways for Gwen to give to causes that align with your church's mission as well as with her passion? Remember that your work with Gwen, and with the other individuals on your path, will take some time to bear fruit. While your team will need to continue to work through the process and remain hopeful and optimistic for the end results, you should not assume that people will respond and grow as quickly as you imagine. Gwen may make subtle changes in her lifestyle, such as bringing her lunch to work instead of going out with colleagues. She may create a list of needed items when planning to shop at the grocery store. She has learned the value of never going grocery shopping when she is hungry.

DREAM

Your team's next task to help Gwen with her finances is to *dream* using this question: **What would happen if giving ten percent of her time, resources, and talents became more meaningful to Gwen?** What would meaningful tithing[89] and giving look like in your church? Are there people in your congregation who can help you *dream* big about giving, such as generous givers and financial planners? How might you re-imagine stewardship by talking about generosity in light of what you learned from Gwen so that others may learn about giving generously? For an example of re-imagining a stewardship campaign, please review Imagine Church's opportunity plan in Chapter 6. After reviewing and brainstorm all of the possibilities, list your *dreams* below.

---

[89] Tithing means giving one-tenth of one's income. The concept is found in Leviticus, Numbers, and Deuteronomy, where the Israelites continue to wander in the wilderness and learn lessons from the Law that will prepare them for life in the Promised Land. Members of every tribe were expected to give a tithe of everything from the land, whether grain from the soil or fruit from the trees, because everything belongs to the LORD. See Leviticus 27:30, NIV.

Given time, your goal will be to help Gwen see a difference in the way she views and uses money. When this occurs, your church will need to *develop* **a plan to make Gwen's experiences of giving ten percent meaningful to her.** Remember, this is the "how" phase of the journey which requires asking how you will create a system for Gwen to tithe so that it is meaningful to her faith and daily life.

List your plans below.

GIVE OUTCOME: GIFTS—GIVING ABOVE AND

You are now close to reaching the goal! When Gwen starts the process of moving away from debt and managing her finances, your path can enable her to give regularly in worship, including giving to special causes and giving ten percent of her income. Your team's goal is to work for a lifelong change in behavior.

DISCERN

As wonderful as this accomplishment might be in the short term for Gwen, your church's long-term giving outcome is to help Gwen **give above ten percent of her time, talents, and resources and to encourage others to give.** To help Gwen move toward sacrificial giving, through a time of prayer and reflection, your team will use this guiding question to *discern* together: **Why would Gwen potentially begin to give above and beyond ten percent?** List the ideas that emerge from your *discernment.*

DREAM

Using the list above, your team will brainstorm ideas of new opportunities that you might create to answer the *dream* question: **What would happen if we created a process that resulted in a genuine life change to inspire a willingness to give back and go the extra mile in giving?** *Dream* big, and resist the urge to say "No, we cannot do this or that." List your dreams below.

DEVELOP

Finally, your team has reached the *develop* phase. Using the guiding *develop* question, work on an action plan, considering this question: **How do we create a process to make Gwen's experience of sacrificial giving more meaningful?** List the steps of your plan below.

After partnering with Gwen on the Give path, we hope she will begin to put into practice your financial strategies to help her manage her finances so that she can reach her *God-dream* of becoming more generous and give sacrificially beyond ten percent.

14

IMPACT

Making a Difference

"But you will receive power when the Holy Spirit comes on you; and you will be my witnesses in Jerusalem, and in all Judea and Samaria, and to the ends of the earth."

Acts 1:8 (NIV)

Too many congregations are invisible or just blend into the landscape. People walk, drive, and jog by the church building, but do not see it as place where things are happening ... people have to get outside the building to make an impact on the community.[90]

F. Douglass Powe, Jr.

Isaac is a 22-year-old unchurched college student who is interested in the Jesus lifestyle. Isaac took a class on World Religions as a sophomore. He was more interested in spirituality than in the church or religion. Isaac

---

[90] F. Douglas Powe, Jr., *New Wine New Wineskins: How African American Congregations Can Reach New Generations* (Nashville: Abingdon Press, 2012), 67-68.

was surprised that he resonated with the story of Jesus. How will your church *discern, dream,* and *develop* practices for Isaac to partner with God and to invite others to explore Jesus' lifestyle? The following exercises will assist you in *discerning, dreaming,* and *developing* a path for Isaac to walk that makes an impact in the lives of others.

THE IMPACT EXERCISES

Starting with Isaac's initial interest in the Jesus lifestyle, your team will create a path to help him learn more about Jesus and the call to become like Him. Once Isaac has completed this step, the next exercise is to practice applying Jesus' teaching to his life. Finally, your task is to help Isaac to invite others to join the Jesus lifestyle.

PRACTICE #1: INTEREST IN THE JESUS LIFESTYLE

To address this concern, your team will need to help Isaac imitate **Practice #1: Learning more about Jesus and accepting the call to be more like Jesus.** Your team will need to *discern* the driving force behind Isaac's interest in Jesus. More specifically, your team will want to listen to the stories about Isaac's experiences in college and what, if anything, he can point to in the class or in his experience that sparked his interest in Jesus. To help your team create a process to hear the stories of new and existing people in your church, it will be helpful for you to introduce open-ended questions for greeting newcomers at church family dinners, in Sunday school classes, other small group opportunities and meetings, and at all volunteer activities. The practice of always asking open-ended questions will help your team model this behavior for your church so that everyone becomes comfortable with communicating by actively listening to others.

DISCERN

In the spaces below, your team will need to begin the *discernment* process by asking **why Isaac wants to change his behavior to live the Jesus lifestyle.** Once you have listened to Isaac, sit together as a team and share about your ideas. Below, list the reasons you heard about why he would like to change.

DREAM

The next step for your team is to *dream:* **What would happen if we made Isaac's experience of the Jesus lifestyle more meaningful?** Below, list the *dreams* from your brainstorming session.

The final step for your team in this part of the process is to answer the *develop* question: **How do we help Isaac by creating a process that will be meaningful to faith and life?** List below the *dreams* from your brainstorming session.

PRACTICE # 2: APPLYING JESUS' TEACHING TO EVERYDAY LIFE

Your team's next step to help Isaac as you move along the path is to *discern, dream,* and *develop* a process that helps him imitate **Practice #2: Applying Jesus' teaching daily.**

DISCERN

Just as before, begin the process by listening to Isaac's stories. Consider the guiding question during your *discernment:* **Why would Isaac apply Jesus' teaching to his life?** What benefits will your team see if Isaac applies this teaching to his life? In the space below, list your responses.

DREAM

As you complete your *discern* list, your team's next step is to engage in the *dream* process. During this brainstorming idea-generating session, your team will need to focus on the following guiding *dream* question: **What would happen if we made learning about Jesus more applicable and inspiring to Isaac's personal life?** List your dreams below.

DEVELOP

Your next task will be to *develop* an action plan to help Isaac apply what he is learning about Jesus' life. Consider the following guiding question:

How do we make Isaac's experience of applying the Jesus lifestyle to his own life more meaningful? List your responses below.

From the results of your work with Isaac, he is becoming more proficient at applying Jesus' teachings to his life.

IMPACT OUTCOME: A WITNESS—INVITE OTHER TO EXPLORE THE JESUS LIFESTYLE.

DISCERN

Next, your team will help Isaac reach the impact outcome of **partnering with God to invite others to explore the Jesus lifestyle.** Consider this *discernment* question: **Why would Isaac potentially move beyond applying Jesus' teaching in his own life to inviting others to explore the Jesus lifestyle?** List all of the reason why Isaac would begin to invite others to explore the Jesus lifestyle?

D R E A M

Taking the list you generated, your next step is to engage the *dream* process. Use the following question to brainstorm with your team: **What would happen if we had a process to guide Isaac to invite others to partner with God in living the Jesus lifestyle?** List your dreams below.

D E V E L O P

Now, you can make your *dreams* a reality and by *developing* an action plan to help make Isaac's experience meaningful. Use this question to guide your development process: **How do we create a plan that helps Isaac to invite others to partner with God?**

List your action plan below.

Through your team's efforts, Isaac has reached the goal of inviting others to explore Jesus' lifestyle. He has become a faithful witness who makes an impact on people's lives. Congratulations! Your church now has completed the discipleship path. Your hard work has paid off, and you now have a discipleship path of practices for people to follow. Additionally, you also have a path to walk that aligns everything your church does to the mission of making disciples.

15

CONCLUSION

Completing the Path

In all my prayers for all of you, I always pray with joy
because of your partnership in the gospel from the first
day until now, being confident of this, that he who began
a good work in you will carry it on to completion until the
day of Christ Jesus.

Philippians 1:4-6, NIV

A disciple is a learner, a student, an apprentice – a practitioner
... disciples of Jesus are people who do not just profess certain
views as their own but apply their growing understanding of
life in the Kingdom of the Heavens to every aspect of their life
on earth.[91]

Dallas Willard

Over the course of the preceding chapters, I have outlined a discipleship
path while at the same time leaving space for your church to figure
out how to clear and walk the path in your own setting. In the process,

---

[91] Dallas Willard, *The Great Omission: Reclaiming Jesus's Essential Teachings on Discipleship* (New York: Harper San Francisco, 2006), 4.

I have aimed to help your church answer the question: *How can we as a church adapt to our current context to reinvent and revitalize ourselves in and for a new time?* Addressing this question by walking the discipleship path is similar to the Israelite journey from oppression to promise and opportunity recorded in the books of Exodus and Numbers. In many ways, there are many parallels between these stories and churches who are struggling with decline and hardships. Like our Israelite counterparts, our churches do not know where we are headed or how we will get there once we determine where "there" is.

Churches are between the proverbial rock and hard place with a sea of uncertainty in front of them and the threat of death through plateau and decline. As a legend from Jewish midrash (commentaries of early Hebrew rabbis on what we call the Old Testament) explains, "God did not separate the impassable Red Sea until the Israelites started to march through it."

Matt Miofsky comments further on the legend and writes,

> **According to the Midrash, Nahshon, the leader of the tribe of Judah, stepped into the roiling waters. He got his feet wet, but the water didn't part. He went in up to his knees, but still nothing. The water hit his waist, and it went nowhere. Then the water went up to his chest, pushing on him and threatening to pull him offshore with the current. But still God did nothing. Finally, Nahshon waded so deep that the water reached his neck. Any further, and he would go under. It was then, when the water threatened to swallow him, when he was literally neck deep, that God showed up.[92]**

Throughout these pages, your church has experienced the courage it takes to walk into an unseparated Red Sea by "clearing and walking" a discipleship path. Though it has not been a quick-fix silver bullet answer for your church, along the way I have offered a process for the journey, with signposts and directions to clear and walk the path.

Revitalizing churches that are experiencing plateau and decline can only happen through processes of *discerning*, *dreaming*, and *developing* a discipleship path that fulfills the church's mission. It is my hope that your

---

[92] Matt Miofsky *Let Go: Leaning Into the Future Without Fear* (Nashville: Abingdon Press, 2019) Kindle Edition, 50.

church has committed to the work of faithfully walking the path. Sure, you will constantly need to clear some debris and neglected overgrowth along your path, but like the path from my childhood neighborhood, the more it is walked, the clearer it remains.

No matter your size or location, you too can *discern, dream,* and *develop* a discipleship path for your church. Thank you for clearing and walking this path with me. I pray that your efforts of *discerning, dreaming,* and *developing* a discipleship path will serve as your guide to connect people with Jesus.

APPENDIX

APPENDIX A

How do you know if your congregation is ready to make disciples? An excellent place to begin is by determining whether this is a public statement commonly heard in your congregation: "We used to have a lot of people in the church, but then ... As a result, things changed, and this has hurt the church."

Another way is to see if your congregation shares any of the following characteristics. If you say yes to four or more, then your church is primed for the assessment.

Statements that Determine Readiness

Our finances have been on a downward spiral for the past three years.

The same people fill the slots for multiple leadership positions.

We are unclear on how to invite and retain new people.

It is a struggle to see a positive future beyond one, three, or five years out.

There are two or three missing generations in attendance.

We cannot replace lost people who used to be engaged or have moved.

167

APPENDIX B

THE READINESS ASSESSMENT [93]

Readiness to create and walk a path of discipleship begins by asking several right questions and taking an honest assessment of your church. Here are the evaluation questions for you to consider:

1. If you ask the clerk at the closest business or school about the name of your church, does he or she recognize it, and can he or she give directions to it?

2. Does your church have a one-percent penetration rate (average number in attendance compared to number of people in the community) of the population within an eight- minute drive of the congregation? [94]

---

[93] Several of the readiness questions are used with permission from the *Certified Transition Guide Cohort of Liminal Space.*

[94] After extensive research on healthy and vital churches in Florida, Dan Jackson has determined this benchmark. For urban centers, Jackson shrinks the radius, and in rural areas, he expands it to typical work drive distances. Dan Jackson is the United Methodist District Superintendent of the Southwest District of the Florida Conference.

3. How has the reality of decline and your love for your church created a sense of urgency to change? What are the signs of support for change?

4. What is your church known for (the significant "sweet spot" story that helps your church differentiate from every other church) that defines your behavior?

5. What is your congregation most proud of (talents, skills, accomplishments, etc.)?

6. When you think about the next five to ten years in the congregation, what excites you most?

7. When you think about the next five to ten years, what scares you most?

8. If you were to stop non-members who regularly drive by your church and ask them what they know about your church, what would they say?

9. If you could only do one ministry outside your church walls, what would it be?

10. How will leaders in your congregation finish the following statement: "We will sabotage our growth process by" (e.g. By procrastinating, making a brash decision, "going it alone," holding on to nostalgia and tradition, etc. List all that apply.)

Answering these questions can be very difficult yet rewarding work. It requires hours of dialogue to determine your church's readiness for a path of discipleship. Each church will be different, but for your church to experience the maximum efficacy, you will need to spend at least a month or more working through the questions and reviewing your answers. I suggest doing this assessment in a retreat setting filled with prayer, reflection, and storytelling. If, at any point you struggle with the questions, then slow down and take the time to work through each one until you have reached common ground. Now, if you are ready, turn the page and let's get started on the path.

APPENDIX C

COMMUNITY ENGAGEMENT QUESTIONNAIRE

The Community Engagement Questionnaire helps to build relationships with people outside the walls of the church. The survey assists the congregation in hearing the stories that are shaping people's identity.

OBJECTIVES

• To help your church better understand its current community so that you can bring hope to those in need.

• To help your church get outside the church walls and build relationships with people in the community so that they will have a vibrant relationship with Jesus.

GIVEAWAYS (OPTIONAL)

Provide information about your church to leave with the respondents. Do not give them everything that your church is doing. The information should not cause information overload to the recipient.

TALKING SCRIPT

Hello! I'm _____. I'm from _____ Church, and we're trying as a church to more effectively meet the needs of our community by conducting a brief survey. Could we have a few minutes of your time to ask five questions?

AGE GROUP OF RESPONDENTS: NUMBER OF CHILDREN:

❑ 18-24   ❑ 25-34   ❑ 35-49   ❑ 50-59   ❑ 60+

NUMBER OF CHILDREN: _____

AGE GROUP OF CHILDREN:

❑ 0-2   ❑ 3-5   ❑ 6-11   ❑ 12-14   ❑ 15-17   ❑ 18-24

QUESTIONS:

1. How long have you lived in this community?

2. What do you think is the greatest need in this community?

3. What are your hopes and dreams for your family?

4. What advice can you give a church on how to provide hope to help families deal with today's pressures?

5. How can we pray for you?

QUESTIONS FOR FUTURE MINISTRY

1. What is the church's passion for the needs discovered from the community assessment (that the congregation brings)?

2. What is the skill set of the congregation (the ability of the congregation to deliver desire)? What does the community need (real opportunities in the community)?

3. What does it look like to bring hope to the community? (The impact on community and church)?

Use the Engagement Guide in Appendix D as the guide to assess themes that emerged from engagement questions. For each section, the X in the yellow box represents an expertise in an area. The open spaces are areas that the church lacks.

APPENDIX D

ENGAGEMENT GUIDE

The Community Engagement Questionnaire helps to build relationships with people outside the walls of the church. The survey assists the congregation in hearing the stories that are shaping people's identity.

VISION VIEW OF FUTURE	PASSION INTEREST *PRESENT*	SKILL ABILITY *PRESENT*	NEED MINISTRY *OPPORTUNITY*	ACTION STRATEGIC *DECISION*
X	X			PRAY BUT DO NOT PURSUE
X		X		AVOID TEMPTATION TO PURSUE
X			X	LET SOMEONE ELSE DO IT
X	X	X		DO NOT FORCE YOUR PASSION AND SKILLS WHERE THERE ISN'T A NEED
X		X	X	OPPORTUNITY TO SERVE BUT NEED TO CONSIDER THE SUSTAINABILITY OF MINISTRY
X	X		X	PRAY FOR GOD TO SEND YOU SKILLED PEOPLE
X	X	X	X	SWEET SPOT TO IMPACT COMMUNITY

CHURCH COMMITMENT   DISTRACTIONS   OPPORTUNITIES

*Engagement guide is used with permission by Ron Carucci, Board Chair and Jon DeWaal, Executive Director of Liminal Space.

**There must be a need to be addressed in the community that fits the church's vision and the church must have the passion and skill to meet the need.

DISCIPLESHIP PATH

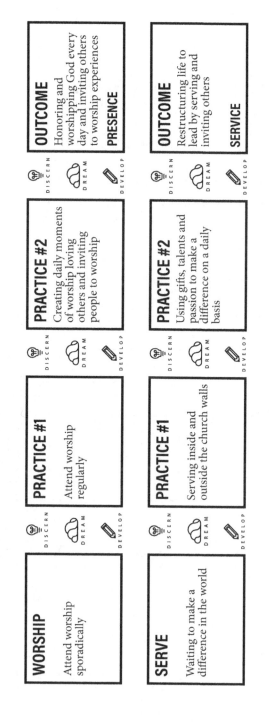

WORSHIP

Attend worship sporadically

DISCERN · DREAM · DEVELOP

PRACTICE #1

Attend worship regularly

DISCERN · DREAM · DEVELOP

PRACTICE #2

Creating daily moments of worship loving others and inviting people to worship

DISCERN · DREAM · DEVELOP

OUTCOME

Honoring and worshipping God every day and inviting others to worship experiences

PRESENCE

SERVE

Waiting to make a difference in the world

DISCERN · DREAM · DEVELOP

PRACTICE #1

Serving inside and outside the church walls

DISCERN · DREAM · DEVELOP

PRACTICE #2

Using gifts, talents and passion to make a difference on a daily basis

DISCERN · DREAM · DEVELOP

OUTCOME

Restructuring life to lead by serving and inviting others

SERVICE

CONTINUED

APPENDIX E

DISCIPLESHIP PATH

GROW

Drawn to God's story and prayer

DISCERN · DREAM · DEVELOP

PRACTICE #1

Becoming closer to God through prayer and Bible study

DISCERN · DREAM · DEVELOP

PRACTICE #2

Daily growing closer to God

DISCERN · DREAM · DEVELOP

OUTCOME

Inviting others to learn spiritual practices to grow closer to God

PRAYER

GIVE

Moving from debt to generosity

DISCERN · DREAM · DEVELOP

PRACTICE #1

Giving occasionally in worship and to special causes

DISCERN · DREAM · DEVELOP

PRACTICE #2

Regular giving 10 percent of recources, time, and talents

DISCERN · DREAM · DEVELOP

OUTCOME

Giving above ten percent and encouraging others to give

GIFTS

IMPACT

Becoming interested in the Jesus life style

DISCERN · DREAM · DEVELOP

PRACTICE #1

Learning more about Jesus and accepting the call to be more like Jesus

DISCERN · DREAM · DEVELOP

PRACTICE #2

Applying Jesus' teaching daily

DISCERN · DREAM · DEVELOP

OUTCOME

Partnering with God to invite others to explore the Jesus life style

WITNESS

179

APPENDIX F

GENEROSITY

Use these steps to assist your team in paying off building debt and deferred maintenance and increase funding for community engagement outreach and mission.

Step 1: Engage the congregation to get 100 percent participation giving. Extra Mile Giving is beyond regular offering.

Step 2: Determine some type of recognition for givers, especially first- and second-time givers.

Step 3: Continue to teach people why and how to tithe.

Step 4: Offer Finance & Debt classes (e.g. Financial Peace) for the congregation

Step 5: Create multiple opportunities to give, (e.g., giving in church, by mail, with text to give, online giving, automatic bank draft).

Step 6: Always tie the offering moment to thanking people for their generosity, explaining how their gifts are an investment in God's future picture for the church (vision-where God's calling you to go).

Step 7: Determine how you will invite people who attend regularly to participating in giving an extra $25 per week for three years.

Step 8: Explain how the bulk of the funding will go toward paying off debt/building and how small incremental percentages (10%, 20%, 30%) will go towards funding community engagement and mission projects.

Step 9: Keep the congregation informed.

Step 10: Celebrate once the goal is achieved.

At each step, your pastor must engage Finance and Trustees teams to get support for extra mile giving.

APPENDIX G

EXTRA-MILE GIVING CHART

BASED ON 200 PAYING $100/ MONTH	% GIVEN	COMMUNITY ENGAGEMENT	% GIVEN	DEBT/BUILDING
200 MEMBERS	$1,200.00			
YEAR 1	$240,000.00	$24,000.00	90	$216,000.00
YEAR 2	$240,000.00	$48,000.00	90	$192,000.00
YEAR 3	$240,000.00	$72,000.00	90	$168,000.00
YEAR 4	$240,000.00	$96,000.00	90	$144,000.00
YEAR 5	$240,000.00	$120,000.00	90	$120,000.00

Suppose your church's indebtedness on its facilities is $285,000.00. In seventeen months of using this process, you will have generated $317,000.00 to pay off the building debt.

After paying off $285,000.00 you will have $32,600 to pay toward any additional deferred maintenance of the church that year. The income generated for the next three years can go toward community engagement and to support another mission which can include your adult, youth and children ministries.

 This format can be adapted to any size church. **Note: An extra $25 per week break downs to $3.57 (less than one grande cafe latte) per day or $100 per month.**

Other Books
from Market Square

marketsquarebooks.com

Wesleyan Grace Theology

Dr. Donald Haynes

From Heaven to Earth Advent Study

Wil Cantrell & Paul Seay

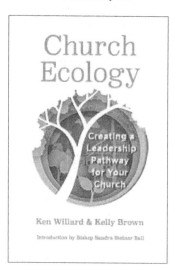

Church Ecology

Creating a Leadership Pathway for your Church

Ken Willard & Kelly Brown

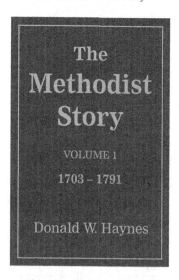

The Methodist Story Volume I ▪ 1703-1791

Dr. Donald Haynes

Grow Your Faith

with these books from Market Square

marketsquarebooks.com

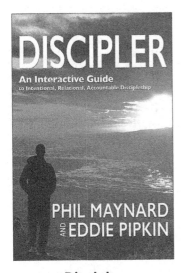

Discipler

Phil Maynard & Eddie Pipkin

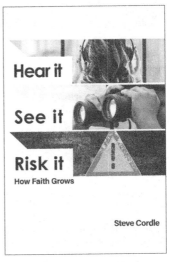

Hear It, See It, Risk It

Steve Cordle

A Christian Teenager's
Guide to Surviving High School

Ashley Conner

Understanding Your Call
11 Biblical Figures Understand
Their Calls from God

by 10 United Methodist Leaders

Grow Your Faith

with these books from Market Square

marketsquarebooks.com

Mission Possible

Kay Kotan & Blake Bradford

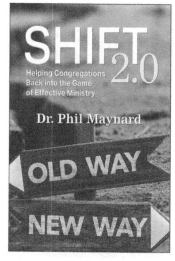

Shift 2.0

Phil Maynard

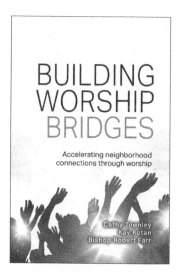

Building Worship Bridges

Cathy Townley

Get Out of That Box!

Anne Bosarge

Latest Titles

from Market Square Books

marketsquarebooks.com

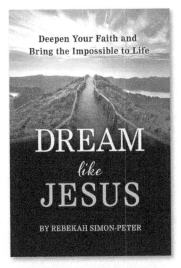

Dream Like Jesus
Bring the Impossible to Life
Rebekah Simon-Peter

From Franchise
To Local Dive
Jason Moore & Roz Picardo

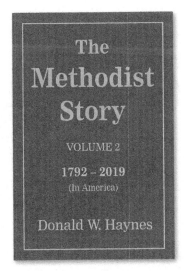

The Methodist Story
Volume 2 ▪ 1792-2019
Dr. Donald W. Haynes

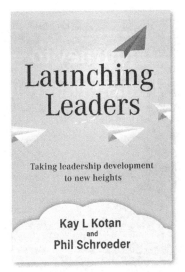

Launching Leaders
Leadership Development
Kay Kotan and Phil Schroeder

Other Books
from Market Square

marketsquarebooks.com

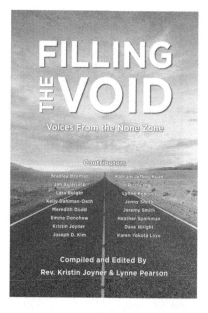

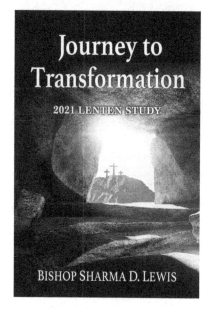